Latin Comprel
for Schools

Martin Hiner

Bristol Classical Press
General Editor: John H. Betts

*To Linda, my long-suffering Head of Department and
Sarah, my longer-suffering wife.*

First published in 2001 by
Bristol Classical Press
an imprint of
Gerald Duckworth & Co. Ltd
61 Frith Street
London W1D 3JL
e-mail: inquiries@duckworth-publishers.co.uk
Website: www.ducknet.co.uk

Reprinted 2002

A catalogue record for this book is available
from the British Library

ISBN 1-85399-623-8

Printed in Great Britain by
Booksprint

PREFACE

There are several books of comprehensions for use up to GCSE, but there is a shortage for the years up to A Level. This volume is intended to fill that gap, though the earlier passages are for use in the period before GCSE. Though grammar and syntax questions are not asked in GCSE, I feel that a true understanding of the language has to be founded on a sound basis of grammar and syntax; only if pupils understand the norm can they appreciate when an author is doing something different, and then ask themselves 'Why?'. Since the principle of Latin word order is based on placing the most important words in the most prominent positions, where questions ask for an explanation of word order I do not consider 'Stress' or 'Emphasis' adequate answers without an explanation of the nature and purpose of the emphasis. Some questions have been asked more as an opportunity for exploration and discussion than in the expectation that most pupils will be able to answer them.

I have tried to produce a body of pieces that I have not found in other books in common use; but a few old favourites have crept in, sometimes because they are such marvellous Latin, and, even after the book was written, examiners have lighted upon one or two of my selected passages. I have kept most of the passages to a length that may be convenient for a prep or for use orally in a lesson, with a few shorter than this, and some later ones longer in the approach to A Level. Any pupil who can tackle some of the later pieces will be well able to face A Level papers!

I am grateful to the Warden and Governors of St Edward's School, Oxford for the sabbatical term during which I wrote most of the book, to Christine Berry for turning my writing into a legible format, and to the Bristol Classical Press for publishing what I hope will prove to be a useful collection.

M J Hiner
Oxford 2000

CONTENTS

How Jason, with the help of the witch, Medea, obtained the golden fleece.

postridie Iason nave prima luce deducta cum sociis profectus ad illum locum iter fecit,   1
ubi Medea **vellus** aureum celatum esse dixerat. quo cum pervenissent, sociis ad mare ad
naves defendendas relictis, ipse cum Medea in silvas contendit. pauca milia passuum
progressi, **vellus**, quod petebant, ex arbore alta suspensum conspexerunt. difficillimum
erat autem id auferre quod **draco** terribilis, flammas ex ore fundens, oculis acribus,   5
arborem custodiebat. at Medea ramum ex arbore proxima raptum **veneno infecit**, quo
draconem faucibus apertis appropinquantem **spargit**, Iasoni clamans ut **vellus** raperet.
ille, dum **draco** somno oppressus humi iacet, procurrit, **vellus** rapit, aufert.
interea socii Iasonis, etiam nunc in ora manentes, animo magis atque magis anxio
reditum eius exspectabant, mirantes num tutus esset rediturus. postquam ad solis   10
occasum frustra exspectaverunt, de eius salute desperare coeperunt.

Line	2 etc	vellus –eris (neut)	fleece
	5 etc	draco –onis	dragon
	6	venenum –i	drug
	6	inficere + acc. + abl.	to dip something into…
	7	fauces –ium	jaws
	7	spargere	to sprinkle

1. At what time did Jason launch his ship?   1
2. To where did Jason and his companions sail?   3
3. How far into the wood was the fleece, and where was it?   3
4. Why was it extremely difficult to remove the fleece?   1
5. What other information are we given about the dragon?   3
6. Explain how Medea overcame the dragon and Jason got the fleece.   5
7. How does the writer bring speed and drama into line 8?   2
8. What were the moods of Jason's companions (a) while they waited, (b) later on?   2,1
9. What are the meanings of *ad* in lines 1, 2 (two meanings) and 10?   4
10. Pick out from the passage: (a) an indirect statement, (b) an indirect
    command, (c) an indirect question, (d) a past participle of a deponent verb,
    (e) a future participle.   5
                                                                                        30

How the Athenians reacted to the news of Xerxes' invasion of Greece.

Xerxes et mari et terra bellum universae inferebat Europae cum tantis copiis, quantas 1
neque antea neque postea habuit **quisquam**. huius enim classis mille et ducentarum
navium longarum fuit, quam duo milia **onerariarum** sequebantur; terrestres autem
exercitus septingentorum milium peditum, equitum quadringentorum milium, fuerunt.
cuius de adventu cum fama in Graeciam pervenisset, et maxime Athenienses oppugnari 5
dicerentur propter pugnam **Marathoniam**, nuntios **Delphos** miserunt ut deum Apollinem
rogarent quid sibi esset faciendum. quibus respondit **Pythia** ut muris **ligneis** se **munirent**.
cum nemo intellegeret quid hoc responsum **vellet**, **Themistocles** Atheniensibus persuasit
hoc esse consilium Apollinis, ut in naves se **suaque** conferrent; eum enim a deo
significari murum **ligneum**. tali consilio probato, **sua** omnia quae moveri poterant 10
Salamina apportant; **arcem** sacerdotibus paucisque maioribus natu tradunt; reliquum
oppidum relinquunt.

Line	2	quisquam (nom)	anybody
	3	navis longa	warship
		oneraria –ae	transport
	6	Marathonius –a –um	of Marathon
		Delphi –orum	Delphi (a town)
	7	Pythia	priestess of Apollo
	7 & 10	ligneus –a –um	wooden
		munire	to protect
	8	velle (here)	to mean
		Themistocles	Themistocles (a leading Athenian)
	9 & 10	sua (neut.pl.)	their belongings
	11	Salamina (acc.)	island of Salamis
		arx arcis	citadel, Acropolis

1. In what way was the army of Xerxes remarkable (lines 1-2)? — 2
2. How many (a) ships (b) land forces in total did Xerxes have? — 4
3. Why were the Athenians in particular thought to be under attack? — 1
4. How did the Athenians respond to the news of Xerxes' arrival? — 4
5. How should *quibus* (7) be translated into idomatic English? — 1
6. Why did the priestess' reply cause a problem? — 2
7. What explanation did Themistocles give of the reply (lines 9-10)? — 3
8. What did the Athenians take to Salamis? — 2
9. Who were left in the city? — 2
10. In what cases are the following words (a) *mari* (1), *omnia* (10), *quae* (10)? — 3
11. Quote from the passage one example each of (a) an ablative absolute, (b) an indirect question, (c) an indirect command, (d) an indirect statement. — 4
12. *exercitus* (4) is an example of a 4th declension noun formed from the past participle or supine of a verb. Find two more nouns of a similar formation. — 2

$$\overline{30}$$

How two oracles were fulfilled.

Laius, rex Thebarum, oraculo quondam certior factus se manu filii sui moriturum esse, 1
iussit puerum suum infantem in monte Cithaerone ad mortem exponi, pedibus **fibula**
transfixis, ne longe a loco **vagari** posset. ibi a **pastore** quodam inventus, Corinthum
adductus est, ubi Oedipus nominatus a rege Polybo educatus est.
multis post annis **aemulus** quidam ira incensus Oedipo negavit eum regis filium esse. 5
Oedipus igitur cum neque a rege neque a regina cognoscere posset cur aemulus hoc
dixisset, Delphos profectus est ad oraculum Apollinis consulendum. deus tamen nihil
respondit nisi 'cave ne patrem occidas.' quo quidem Oedipus tam graviter permotus est
ut Corinthi diutius habitare nollet; credebat enim Polybum patrem esse. dum autem
Thebas iter facit, seni cuidam in via occurrit, qui cum servo Delphos **curru** vehebatur. 10
servus, ubi Oedipum conspexit, magna voce clamat ut de via excedat, et senex Oedipum
stimulo percutit. ille igitur iratus et senem deiectum et servum interficit, nesciens se
patrem suum Laium occidere.

Line 2	fibula –ae	pin	Names	
3	vagari	to wander	Thebae –arum	Thebes
	pastor –is	shepherd	Delphi –orum	Delphi
5	aemulus –i	rival	Both cities in Greece	
10	currus –us	chariot		
12	stimulus –i	goad (for driving horses)		

1. What was Laius told by an oracle?   1
2. What instructions did Laius give (to *exponi*)? Why did Laius have the feet   3, 2
    pinned together?
3. Lines 5-7: explain why Oedipus went to Delphi.   4
4. Translate the god's reply.   2
5. How must *nisi* (8) and *quo* (8) be translated in idiomatic English in these
    contexts?   2
6. Why would Oedipus not return to Corinth?   2
7. Recount what happened on the journey to Thebes, and explain how the oracles
    were fulfilled.   6
8. Why are (a) *facit* (10), (b) *clamat* (11) in the present tense?   2
9. Account for the cases of *Corinthum* (3) and *Corinthi* (9).   2
10. Choose from the text and put down the line reference for one example each of
    (a) a consecutive (result) clause, (b) a final (purpose) clause, (c) an indirect
    question, (d) an indirect command, (e) an ablative absolute.   5
11. Distinguish between *quondam* (1), *quodam* (3), *quidem* (8), *cuidam* (10).   4
      35

Hannibal, in flight from the Romans, had taken refuge with Antiochus, king of Syria, who was then himself defeated by the Romans.

Hannibal, Antiocho fugato, quod timebat ne hostibus traderetur, ad Cretam navem solvit   1
et statim **Gortynam** equitavit. quo cum advenisset, sensit se magno fore in periculo
propter **avaritiam** Gortyniorum; multam enim secum pecuniam portabat, de qua sciebat
exisse **famam**. itaque tale consilium capit. amphoras complures complet **plumbo**, summas
tegit auro et argento. has praesentibus urbis principibus in templo Dianae deponit,   5
simulans se suas fortunas illorum **fidei** credere. tum statuas **aeneas**, quas secum portabat,
omnes sua pecunia complet easque in **propatulo** domi ponit. ubi Hannibal tandem ab urbe
discedere constituit, Gortynii templum magna cura custodiunt, non **tam** a ceteris **quam**
ab Hannibale, ne ille eis inscientibus amphoras auferret secumque duceret. sic Hannibal
suas res conservavit.   10

Line	2	Gortyna	Gortyn, a city in Crete
	3	avaritia	greed
	4	fama	news
		plumbum –i	lead
	6	fides –ei	honesty
		aeneus –a –um	made of bronze
	7	propatulum	forecourt
	8	tam … quam	so much … as

1.	Of what was Hannibal afraid?	2
2.	To whom does *hostibus* (1) refer?	1
3.	How did Hannibal travel from Syria to Gortyn?	2
4.	*quo* (2): how should this be translated in idiomatic English?	1
5.	Why was Hannibal worried about the greed of the people of Gortyn?	2
6.	Lines 4-5: what did Hannibal do with the jars?	4
7.	Why does Hannibal have the leading citizens of Gortyn with him in the temple?	3
8.	What part do the bronze statues play in the story?	2
9.	Why were the people of Gortyn guarding the temple?	3
10.	Give an appropriate word to translate *res* in line 10.	1
11.	Give an example of where Nepos uses word order to emphasise a particular word.	1
12.	What part of what verbs are *fugato* (1), *fore* (2), *exisse* (4)?	3
		25

*In the reign of Servius, sixth king of Rome (trad. 578-535 BC) the Romans and Sabines
are in a power struggle. Rome is clearly gaining the upper hand, but one Sabine finds
a way to settle the struggle in favour of the Sabines.*

bos in Sabinis cuidam agricolae nata esse dicitur miranda magnitudine et specie, quae   1
sacra putabatur. oraculum vero cecinerant **vates**, cuius civitatis civis eam Dianae
sacrificavisset, in ea civitate futurum esse imperium; idque oraculum, et huic agricolae
Sabino notum, etiam ad sacerdotem templi Dianae, quod Romae erat, pervenerat.
Sabinus igitur, ut prima dies sacrificio apta visa est, bovem Romam actam ad templum   5
Dianae deducit, ut sacrificaret. ibi sacerdos, et admiratione victimae motus et oraculi
memor, Sabinum ita adloquitur: 'quid tu, hospes, facere paras?' inquit, 'num **inceste**
sacrificium Dianae facies? tu ante **vivo** flumine te **perfundere** debes; in ima valle fluit
Tiberis.' Sabinus, religione tactus, qui omnia **rite** facta cuperet, statim ad **Tiberim**
descendit; interea Romanus sacrificat Dianae bovem. id mire gratum regi atque civitati fuit.   10

Line	1	bos bovis	heifer, young cow
	2	vates –is	seer, prophet
	7	memor –ris + gen	mindful of, remembering
		inceste (adverb)	without being purified
	8	vivus	flowing
		perfundere	to bathe
	9	Tiberis –is (acc. Tiberim)	the River Tiber
		rite (adverb)	rightly, with proper ceremony

1.   What are we told in the first sentence about the heifer?   4
2.   What oracle had the prophets proclaimed?   4
3.   Of what verb is *cecinerant* (2) a part?   1
4.   When did the farmer take the heifer to the temple?   2
5.   What were the thoughts of the priest when he saw the heifer?   2
6.   Explain how the priest got the farmer to leave the temple.   3
7.   Why did the farmer do as the priest suggested?   2
8.   Why did the priest get the farmer to leave the temple? How did the king and
     the Romans feel about his action?   2
9.   Account for the cases of *Romae* (4) and *Romam* (5).   2
10. Distinguish the uses of *ut* in lines 5 and 6.   2
11. How can you tell from this passage the gender of *templum*?   1
                                                                    ___
                                                                    25

5

Pliny, VI. 24.

Pliny tells the story of a suicide pact, observing that a noble deed of an obscure person passes almost unnoticed.

nuper cum per **lacum Larium** navigarem, senex quidam ostendit mihi villam cuius 1
cubiculum in lacum prominebat. 'ex hoc', inquit, 'olim **municeps nostra** cum marito se
praecipitavit.' mihi roganti cur hoc illa fecisset, 'maritus,' inquit, 'gravissimo morbo
affectus erat. femina eum rogavit ut permitteretur corpus inspicere; negavit enim
quemquam ei fidelius dicturum esse num sanari posset. vidit, desperavit. maritum 5
imploravit ut simul morerentur. igitur se cum marito **ligavit** abiecitque in lacum'.

ego, quamquam municeps sum, de hoc facto numquam antea audiveram; non **quia**
factum non clarum, sed **quia** illa ingloria erat quae fecit. 8

Line	1	lacus Larius	Lake Como
	2	municeps nostra	a woman from our town
	5	quisquam	anybody
	6	ligare	to tie
	7 & 8	quia	because

1. What was Pliny doing when he heard this story? 1
2. What did the old man show him, and what did he say had taken place there? 4
3. What does Pliny ask the old man? 1
4. What did the wife ask of her husband, and what reason for this request is given in lines 3-4? 3,2
5. Express in English direct speech what the wife says to her husband in lines 4-5 (*negavit* to *posset*). 5
6. Lines 5-6: What does the wife ask her husband? Why does she ask this? 2
7. How does the old man's story end? 2
8. Why is Pliny surprised that he had not heard this story before? 1
9. How does he account for this, and what reason does he reject? 2
10. What parts of what verbs are *roganti* (3), *morerentur* (6)? 2

    25

6

Ulysses' men go into the house of the witch Circe, leaving Eurylochus on watch outside.

Circe ingressis sociis **baculo** suo aureo capita eorum leviter tetigit; quo facto, omnes 1
subito in porcos sunt conversi. interea Eurylochus, nesciens quid in villa ageretur, ad
portam anxio animo exspectabat dum exirent; postquam tamen ad solis occasum frustra
ibi moratus est, constituit solus ad navem regredi. quo cum tandem pervenisset, adeo
timore permotus est ut **Ulixi** quid accidisset roganti non lucide narrare posset. at **Ulixes** 5
satis intellexit socios suos in periculo esse et ad **Circes** villam properavit. ei autem villam
intraturo occurrit deus Mercurius qui **herbam** magicam ei dedit: 'hanc cape', inquit, 'et,
cum **Circe** te **baculo** tanget, tu, gladio stricto, fac impetum in eam.'
    Ulixes, ut villam intravit, ab ipsa **Circe** benigne exceptus, ad cenam invitatus.
quamquam cibus **veneno** infectus est, tanta erat vis illius **herbae** quam dederat Mercurius 10
ut nec **veneno Ulixes** laederetur, neque in porcum conversus sit postquam **Circe** eum
baculo tetigit. at ille statim **Circen** oppugnat, facile superat, suos in formam humanam
reddere cogit.

Line	1 etc	Circe: acc. Circen, gen. Circes, abl. Circe	
	1 etc	baculum −i	wand
	5 etc	Ulixes −is	Ulysses
	7 & 10	herba −ae	herb
	10 & 11	venenum −i	poison

1. How did Circe turn Ulysses' men into pigs?   2
2. Why was Eurylochus anxious?   2
3. How should these words be translated in their contexts into idiomatic English: *ad* (2), *ad* (3), *quo* (1), *quo* (4)?   4
4. What was the result of Eurylochus' fear after he returned to the ship?   4
5. Where was Ulysses when Mercury met him?   2
6. What instructions did Mercury give Ulysses?   5
7. How did Circe show Ulysses that he was welcome?   2
8. What was the effect of the magic herb that Mercury had given Ulysses?   3
9. How does the author bring a sense of dramatic action into the last sentence?   2
10. Pick out from the passage the present infinitive and perfect participle of *gradior* in compounds.   2
11. What are the meanings or constructions of *ut* in lines 9 and 11? ("That" and "so that" are not adequate answers.)   2

                                          30

When the Alexandrians try to block Caesar's advance, they are decisively defeated.
The king is Ptolemy, king of Egypt.

inter castra regis et Caesaris iter flumen intercedebat angustum, altissimis ripis, quod in   1
Nilum influebat; aberat autem ab regis castris milia passuum circiter septem. rex cum hoc
itinere venire Caesarem cognovisset, equitatum omnem **expeditos**que delectos pedites ad
flumen misit qui transitu Caesarem prohiberent. sed equites Caesaris partim disperserunt
ut **vada** fluminis quaererent, partim flumen tranaverunt et legionarii, magnis arboribus   5
excisis, quae longitudine utramque ripam contingerent, et proiectis, flumen transierunt.
quorum impetum adeo pertimuerunt hostes, ut in fuga spem salutis collocarent; sed id
frustra; namque ex ea fuga pauci ad regem refugerunt, paene omni reliqua multitudine
interfecta. Caesar protinus victor ad castra regis contendit. at Alexandrini, sui servandi
causa, statim legatos emiserunt ad pacem petendam.   10

Line 3	expeditus	light-armed
5	vada –orum	shallows, ford
6	excidere	to cut down

1. Lines 1-2 contain five pieces of information about the river. What are they?   5
2. What does *cum* mean in line 2?   1
3. What information did the king get, and how did he react to it?   2,4
4. How did (a) the cavalry (b) the infantry get across the river?   3,3
5. What is the force of the prefix *per-* on *pertimuerunt* (7)?   1
6. Lines 7-8: insert an appropriate verb and translate *sed id frustra*. To what
    does *id* refer?   2,1
7. How successfully did the Alexandrians try to escape?   4
8. What are the gender, number and case of *omni* (8)?   1
9. Quote from the passage one example of (a) a consecutive (result) clause, (b)
    an indirect statement, (c) an ablative absolute, (d) a connecting relative.   4
10. This passage contains examples of four ways of expressing purpose. What are
    they?   4
                                                                                    ──
                                                                                    35

How Ulysses killed the suitors.

Ulixi, regi Ithacae, erat uxor fidelissima, Penelope. cum ille Troia capta domum non 1
reverteretur neque per multos annos ulla de eo fama Ithacam perveniret, multi principes e
finitimis insulis Ithacam convenerunt, reginam in matrimonium petentes. quibus
Penelope, cum eos **depellere** non posset, haec dixit, se nemini **nubere** velle donec **pallium**
confecisset quam nuper **texere** incepisset. interea, ut tempus quam diutissime traheret, 5
quodcumque cotidie **texebat**, nocte clam **retexebat**. principes autem, cum dolum
cognovissent, postulaverunt ut finem morandi faceret. illa igitur certamen instituit; e
cubiculo suo magnum effert **arcum** quem Ulixes quondam gerere solitus erat. 'si quis'
inquit 'hunc arcum **intendere** poterit, illi nubam. '**arcus** autem tam rigidus erat ut nemo
principum eum **flectere** posset. at Ulixes, forte hoc ipso die domum regressus, **arcu** facile 10
flexo, principes omnes sagittis morti dedit. sic regnum suum et fidelem uxorem post
viginiti annos recepit.

Line	1	Ulixes –is	Ulysses
	4	depellere	to get rid of
		nubere + dat.	to marry
		pallium –i	cloak
	5 & 6	texere	to weave
	6	retexere	to unravel
	8 etc	arcus –us	bow
	9	intendere	to bend, string
	10 & 11	flectere, flexum	to bend

1. Why might Penelope have believed that Ulysses was dead? 2
2. Why did the chiefs come from neighbouring islands to Ithaca? 2
3. Under what circumstances does Penelope say she would be prepared to marry again? 2
4. What trick did she play, and why did she play it? 3,2
5. Translate *postulaverunt ut finem morandi faceret* (7). What construction is *ut* introducing here? 2,1
6. What were the conditions of the contest which Penelope arranged? 2
7. Lines 10-11 *arcu facile flexo*: what information has previously been given about Ulysses and the bow which would explain this? 3
8. What did Ulysses do after stringing the bow? 2
9. How long had he been away? 1
10. Give the 1st person singular of the present indicative of *incepisset* (5), *solitus erat* (8), *regressus* (10). 3
11. Account for the cases of *Ulixi* (1), *Troia* (1), *principum* (10). 3
12. Account for the subjunctives *incepisset* (5), *posset* (10). 2
  30

9

Nepos, *Hannibal* XXIII. 12.

183 BC Hannibal, in flight from the Romans, has secretly taken refuge with Prusias, king of Bithynia.

interea legati **Prusiae** Romae erant et olim apud Quinctium Flaminium cenaverunt; ex 1
quibus unus forte dixit Hannibalem in Prusiae regno esse. id postero die Flaminius
senatui nuntiavit. **patres,** qui existimabant Hannibale vivo pacem numquam futuram
esse, legatos in Bithyniam miserunt qui regem rogarent ne hostem suum secum haberet
sibique dederet. Prusia his **negare** non ausus est. 5
Hannibal autem in castello, in quo habitabat, ei a rege dato, in omnibus partibus **exitus**
fecerat, ne umquam ibi a Romanis **obsideretur.** quo cum legati Romanorum venissent ac
multitudine militum **circumdedissent,** servus quidam, ab ianua prospiciens, Hannibali
dixit plurimos armatos apparere. ille anxius ei imperavit ut omnes partes aedificii
circumiret ac sibi nuntiaret num eodem modo undique **obsideretur.** cum puer omnes 10
exitus occupatos esse renuntiavisset, Hannibal sensit se oppugnari, ac **venenum,** quod
hoc timens semper secum habere solebat, sumpsit.

Line	1	Prusia –ae		Prusias
	3	pater patris		senator
	5	negare		to say 'no'
	6 & 11	exitus –us		exit, way out
	7 & 10	obsidere		to blockade, besiege
	8	circumdare		to surround
	11	venenum –i		poison

1. What information did one of the envoys of Prusias give Flaminius, and on what occasion did he give it? 2,1
2. What request did the Roman senate make of king Prusias? What was their reason for making this request (3-4)? 3,3
3. What information are we given about the stronghold in which Hannibal was living? Why had Hannibal made changes to the stronghold? 3,2
4. What did the slave tell Hannibal that he could see? 2
5. How did Hannibal feel about this report, and what did he tell the slave to do? 1,5
6. What did the slave report this time? 2
7. Why did Hannibal always have poison with him? 2
8. Quote from the passage one example each of (a) an indirect question, (b) a locative, (c) a final (purpose) clause, (d) a semi-deponent verb. 4
                                                                             30

Thales gives Solon a practical demonstration of his reason for remaining a bachelor.
Thales lives in Miletus in modern Turkey.

Solon, vir omnium Atheniensium sapientissimus, dum apud Thalem **commoratur,** 1
hospitem suum rogavit cur uxorem ducere, gignere liberos nollet. cui Thales non statim
respondit, sed, quo facilius Solon causam intellegeret, paulo post iussit **peregrinum**
quendam nuntiare se Athenis nuper advenisse. hic Soloni num quid novi ibi fieret roganti
respondit, ut Thales imperaverat, 'nihil; sed multi **dolebant** quia iuvenis quidam, patre 5
clarissimo natus, mortuus erat; neque pater aderat cum **foris** iter tum faceret.' tum Solon
quod nomen patri esset rogavit; sed **peregrinus** negavit se nomen meminisse posse,
quamquam omnes sapientiam illius laudavissent. quo audito, Solon multum perturbatus
'Solonisne filius', inquit, 'erat is qui periit?' 'Solonis vero.' tum adeo dolore motus est ut
Thales subridens 'sis bono animo' dixerit; 'nam haec non vere sunt relata. at ea quae et 10
Solonem in tantum terrorem possunt conicere mihi persuadent ne sim pater.'

Line 2	commorari	to stay
3 & 7	peregrinus –i	stranger
5	dolere	to mourn
6	foris (adverb)	abroad

1. What did Solon ask Thales? 3
2. Translate *quo facilius Solon causam intellegeret* (3). 3
3. What did Thales tell the stranger to do? 2
4. Translate *num quid novi ibi fieret* (4). 2
5. What does *ut* (5) mean? What indication does the Latin give that it means this? 2
6. What clues in the conversation that follows (5-8) lead Solon to suspect that the dead boy is his son? 3
7. Translate *sis bono animo* (10) into idiomatic English, and account for the subjunctive. 2
8. Explain in your own words Thales' reason for not wishing to be a father. 2
9. Account for the cases of *novi* (4), *roganti* (4), *patri* (7). 3
10. Why are the following verbs subjunctive: *laudavissent* (8), *dixerit* (10), *sim* (11)? 3
    25

11

After a series of troop movements, Hannibal moves on Grumentum, and a Roman army moves on Hannibal.

itaque ne cum duobus exercitibus simul confligeret, Hannibal nocte castra ex agro 1
Tarentino movit atque in Bruttios concessit. Claudius consul in Sallentinos agmen
convertit; Hostilius Capuam petens obvius ad Venusiam fuit Claudio. ibi ex utroque
exercitu electa peditum quadraginta milia, duo milia et quingenti equites, quibus consul
adversus Hannibalem rem gereret: reliquas copias Hostilius Capuam ducere iussus, ut Q. 5
Fulvio proconsuli traderet.
Hannibal undique contracto exercitu, quem in hibernis aut in praesidiis habuerat, ad
Grumentum venit spe recipiendi oppida quae per metum ad Romanos **defecissent**. eodem
a Venusia consul Romanus contendit, et mille fere et quingentos passus castra ab hoste
locat. Grumenti moenibus prope iniunctum videbatur **Poenorum** vallum; quingenti passus 10
intererant. castra **Punica** ac Romana interiacebat campus; colles imminebant nudi sinistro
lateri Carthaginiensium, dextro Romanorum.

Line	2	Tarentinus –a –um	of Tarentum (a city)
	8	deficere	to change sides
	10	Poeni –orum	Carthaginians
	11	Punicus –a –um	Carthaginian

1. Why did Hannibal move his camp? — 2
2. Lines 3-5: what forces were picked from the two armies, and what was their purpose? — 2,2
3. Capua and Venusia are both towns. Explain why *Capuam* (5) has no pre-position, while *Venusiam* (3) is preceded by *ad*. — 2
4. In lines 5-6 what instructions are given to Hostilius? — 3
5. What forces did Hannibal gather together, and why did he head towards Grumentum? — 2,3
6. Draw a simple sketch to show (a) Grumentum, (b) Hannibal's camp, (c) Claudius' camp, (d) the plain, (e) the hills. Mark in the distances given in the text. — 6
7. What would be appropriate translations in their contexts for (a) *ager* (1), (b) *peto* (3), (c) *nudus* (11)? — 3
8. In what cases are the following words, and why are they in these cases: *nocte* (1), *Claudio* (3), *peditum* (4), *passus* (9)? — 4
9. Give the present infinitive active of *electa* (4), *contracto* (7), *intererant* (11). — 3
10. What are the meanings of *uterque* (3) and *undique* (7)? What is the force or meaning of the suffix *-que*? — 3

35

Cicero, *Pro Cluentio* 9. 26-28.

Sassia is a widow, sought in marriage by Oppianicus. She raises an unexpected objection, for which he has a simple and decisive remedy.

Oppianicus, divitiarum eius cupidus, Sassiam, cuius virum ipse occiderat, in 1
matrimonium ducere cupivit. petit ut sibi Sassia **nubat**; illa autem non illam Oppianici
domum, viri sui sanguine **redundantem, reformidat**, sed quod haberet duo ille filios,
idcirco se ab his **nuptiis** abhorrere respondit. domi ille habebat infantem filium; alter eius
filius **Teani** apud **matrem** educabatur, quem subito sine causa **Teano** arcessit. mater nihil 5
mali suspicans mittit, atque eo ipso die puer, cum hora undecima in publico valens visus
esset, ante noctem mortuus, et postridie, antequam luceret, combustus est. dies nondum
decem intercesserant, cum ille alter filius infans necatur. itaque **nubit** statim Oppianico
Sassia; nec mirum est, cum se non nuptialibus donis sed filiorum funeribus **delenitam**
videret. ita **quod** ceteri propter liberos pecuniae cupidi solent esse, ille propter pecuniam 10
liberos amittere **iucundius** esse putavit.

Line	2 & 8	nubere + dat.	to marry
	3	redundare	to overflow
		reformidare	to shrink from
	4	idcirco	for that reason
		nuptiae –arum	marriage
	5	Teanum –i	Teanum, a town
		matrem	Oppianicus divorced his first wife
	9	delenire	to woo
	10	quod	whereas
	11	iucundus –a –um	pleasant

1. Why did Oppianicus want to marry Sassia, and why might one have expected her to refuse? — 1,2
2. What grounds did Sassia give for refusing marriage? — 2
3. Explain the cases of *Teani* and *Teano* (5). — 2
4. *nihil mali suspicans* (5-6): what case is *mali* and why is it in this case? Why might the mother have been suspicious? — 2
5. Relate what happened to the boy after his mother sent him, expressing timing in modern terms. — 6
6. When did the other boy die (7-8)? — 1
7. Why was it not surprising that Sassia at once married Oppianicus? — 4
8. Express the point of the last sentence (10-11) in your own words. — 4
9. Compare the meanings of and constructions following *cum* in lines 6, 8 and 9. — 3
10. Account for the subjunctive uses in *nubat* (2), *haberet* (3), *luceret* (7). — 3
11. Comment on Cicero's use of alliteration in this passage. — 5

35

55 BC Caesar has brought his army back from Britain to Gaul, but two transport ships fail to make it to the harbour and are swept further down the coast.

quibus ex navibus cum essent expositi milites circiter trecenti atque in castra 1
contenderent, Morini, quos Caesar in Britanniam proficiscens **pacatos** reliquerat, spe
praedae adducti primo non ita magno suorum numero circumsteterunt ac, si se interfici
nollent, arma ponere iusserunt. cum illi **orbe** facto se defenderent, celeriter ad clamorem
circiter sex milia hominum convenerunt. qua re nuntiata, Caesar omnem ex castris 5
equitatum suis auxilio misit. interea nostri milites impetum hostium sustinuerunt atque
amplius horis quattuor fortissime pugnaverunt et, paucis vulneribus acceptis, complures
ex hostibus occiderunt. postquam vero equitatus noster in conspectum venit, hostes
abiectis armis terga verterunt magnusque eorum numerus est occisus.   9

Line 2	pacare	to pacify
4	orbis –is	ring, circle

1. How many soldiers had been on the transports, and what were they doing when the Morini surrounded them?   2
2. Why was an attack by the Morini unexpected, and what had led them to attack?   2,2
3. What do the Morini say to the Roman troops? Why is *nollent* (4) subjunctive?   3,1
4. Lines 4-5: how many Morini were attracted by the shouting?   2
5. Lines 5-9: what information do these lines give us about the battle and the casualties on both sides?   8
6. In what cases are these words, and why are they in these cases: *hominum* (5), *suis* (6), *auxilio* (6), *horis* (7)?   4
7. Using examples from this passage of participles in the nominative, accusative and ablative, explain when an ablative absolute should or should not be used.   6
                                                                                    30

109 BC In the war against Jugurtha, king of the Numidians, Metellus had put the enemy to flight, but suffered heavy losses in the process. So, he now changes his tactics, initially with some success.

Metellus in eisdem castris quattuor dies moratus, **saucios** cum cura reficit, omnes in   1
contione laudat atque agit gratias. interea tamen **transfugas** misit qui explorarent ubi esset
Jugurtha et quid ageret, utrum cum paucis esset an exercitum haberet. at rex in loca
saltuosa et natura munita se receperat ibique cogebat exercitum numero hominum
ampliorem sed infirmum. **id ea gratia eveniebat quod** praeter regios equites nemo   5
omnium Numidarum ex fuga regem sequitur. igitur Metellus ubi videt regem bellum
renovare, et minore **detrimento** hostes vinci quam suos vincere, statuit non proeliis sed
alio modo bellum esse gerendum. itaque in Numidiae loca **opulentissima** progressus,
agros vastat atque, multis castellis et oppidis captis incensisque, cives aut interfici iubet
aut militibus donat. quae res multo magis quam proelium regem terrebant, adeo ut   10
consilium quod optimum videbatur caperet; reliquo exercitu in eisdem locis manere
iusso, ipse cum delectis equitibus Metellum nocte secutus, Romanos subito aggressus est.
eorum plerique cadunt, multi capiuntur, nemo omnium intactus profugit.

Line	1	saucius –a –um	wounded
	2	contio –onis	assembly
		transfuga –ae	deserter
	4	saltuosus –a –um	wooded
	5	id ea gratia eveniebat quod	this was due to the fact that …
	7	detrimentum –i	losses, casualties
	8	opulentus –a –um	rich

1.	What does Metellus do to restore his army physically and mentally?	3
2.	What information does Metellus want the deserters to get?	4
3.	Why are *explorarent* (2) and *esset* (2) subjunctive?	2
4.	What cases are *natura* and *munita* (4)?	2
5.	What are we told about the army which Jugurtha was gathering, and what was the reason for this?	2,3
6.	Line 7 *statuit*: what decision did Metellus take, and what were the reasons for this decision?	3,3
7.	What was Metellus's new strategy?	6
8.	How did this strategy affect Jugurtha?	2
9.	Lines 10-11: translate *adeo* to *caperet*.	3
10.	What was Jugurtha's plan?	4
11.	What was the outcome for the Romans of Jugurtha's attack?	3
		40

Cicero, *In Verrem* II. IV. 46. 103.

Cicero tells the jury at a trial about the plundering of a very holy shrine on the island of Malta.

insula est Melita, indices, satis lato a Sicilia mari periculosoque diiuncta, in qua est eodem 1
nomine oppidum. ab eo oppido non longe in promonturio **fanum** est Iunonis antiquum,
quod tanta religione semper fuit, ut non modo illis Punicis bellis, quae in his fere locis
navali copia gesta sunt, sed etiam **hac praedonum** multitudine semper inviolatum
sanctumque fuerit. etiam **fama est**, classe quondam Masinissae regis ad eum locum 5
adpulsa, imperatorem regis dentes **eburneos** incredibili magnitudine e **fano** sustulisse et
eos in Africam portavisse Masinissaeque donavisse. rex primo delectatus est; post, ubi
audivit unde essent, statim homines in nave misit, qui eos dentes reponerent. 8

Line 2 & 6	fanum –i	shrine
4	hac	in this area
	praedo –onis	pirate
5	fama est	there is a story that ...
6	adpellere	to bring to land
	eburneus –a –um	of ivory

1. What are we told about the sea that separates Malta from Sicily? 2
2. Say as precisely as you can where the shrine of Juno was. 2
3. How does Cicero emphasise the reverence with which the shrine was regarded? 4
4. Give the gender, number and case of (a) *quae* (3), (b) *navali* (4). 4
5. What would we call *dentes eburneos* (6), and what was remarkable about the ones in this story? 2
6. What part is played in the story by the admiral of the king's fleet? 3
7. What was the king's initial reaction to the gift? 1
8. Why did he change his mind, and what did he do as a result of this change of mind? 2,2
9. Why are the following verbs in the subjunctive (a) *fuerit* (5), (b) *essent* (8), (c) *reponerent* (8)? 3

25

396 BC When news comes to Sparta that the Persian king, Artaxerxes, is preparing to invade Greece, Agesilaus decides to strike first.

Agesilaus, simul ac rex **Lacedaemoniorum** factus est, eis persuasit ut exercitus emitterent   1
in Asiam bellumque regi Artaxerxi facerent, docens melius esse in Asia quam in Europa
bellum gerere. namque fama exierat Artaxerxem comparare classes pedestresque
exercitus quos in Graeciam mitteret. data **potestate**, tanta celeritate usus est ut in Asiam
cum copiis pervenerit priusquam duces Persarum scirent eum profectum esse.   5
        itaque Tissaphernes, qui summum imperium tum inter duces Persarum habebat,
copiis nondum paratis, simulans se nuntios ad **regem** de pace missurum esse, **indutias** ab
Agesilao petivit. iuravit uterque se pacem tres menses sine perfidia conservaturum esse.
in qua **pactione** summa fide mansit Agesilaus; Tissaphernes tamen nihil aliud quam
bellum comparavit. Agesilaus, quamquam haec intellegebat, **iusiurandum** servabat   10
dicebatque Tissaphernem **periurio** suo deos sibi iratos facere, se autem et exercitum
validiorem facere et deos amiciores, quod eis favere solerent quos fidem conservare
viderent.

Line	1	Lacedaemonii –orum	Spartans
	4	potestas –tatis	permission
	7	rex regis	the king of Persia
		indutiae –arum	truce
	9	pactio –onis	agreement
	10	iusiurandum iurisiurandi	oath
	11	periurium –ii	perjury, breaking of an oath

1. What did Agesilaus persuade the Spartans to do, and what was his reasoning
    behind this?   2,2
2. What forces was Artaxerxes preparing?   2
3. How does Nepos emphasise the speed of Agesilaus' crossing to Asia?   3
4. Line 6: what was the position of Tissaphernes?   1
5. Why did Tissaphernes ask Agesilaus for a truce, and what reason did he give
    Agesilaus for one?   2,2
6. To whom does *uterque* (8) refer?   1
7. Contrast the behaviour of Agesilaus and Tissaphernes in lines 9-10.   3
8. What results does Agesilaus foresee from their differing behaviour, and what
    reason does he give for this?   3,2
9. What parts of what verbs are *profectum esse* (5) and *missurum esse* (7)?   2
10. Account for the subjunctives *emitterent* (1), *mitteret* (4), *pervenerit* (5),
    scirent (5), *solerent* (12).   5
                                                                                   ──
                                                                                   30

In Africa Curio, Caesar's general, has been killed along with all his infantry by the army of Juba, king of Numidia, who is helping Pompey's general, Varus. A few cavalry escaped the slaughter and reported it in Curio's camp.

his rebus cognitis Marcius Rufus quaestor in castris relictus a Curione cohortatur suos, ne   1
animo deficiant. illi orant atque obsecrant ut in Siciliam navibus reportentur. pollicetur
magistrisque imperat navium ut primo vespere omnes **scaphas** ad litus appulsas habeant.
sed tantus fuit omnium terror ut alii adesse copias Iubae dicerent, alii cum legionibus
instare Varum iamque se pulverem venientium cernere, quarum rerum nihil omnino   5
acciderat, alii classem hostium celeriter advolaturum suspicarentur. itaque perterritis
omnibus sibi quisque consulebat. qui in classe erant proficisi properabant. horum fuga
navium onerariarum magistros incitabat: pauci **lenunculi** ad officium imperiumque
conveniebant. sed tanta erat completis litoribus **contentio**, qui potissimum ex magno
numero conscenderent, ut multitudine atque onere non nulli deprimerentur, reliqui hoc   10
timore propius adire tardarentur.

Line	3	scapha –ae	small boat, cutter
	8	navis oneraria	transport
		lenunculus –i	small sailing-boat, skiff
	9	contentio –onis	dispute

1.   What are the reactions to the news of (a) Rufus (b) the troops?   2,2
2.   What instructions does Rufus give to the ships' captains?   2
3.   What were the rumours and fears of the soldiers in the camp?   5
4.   Translate *sibi quisque consulebat* (7). What does *consulo* mean when followed
     by an accusative?   2,1
5.   Lines 7-8: how did most of the fleet react (to *incitabat*)?   2
6.   What does *ad* mean in line 8?   1
7.   About what was the dispute on the shore, and what was the result?   2,4
8.   *multitudine atque onere* (10) is an example of an hendiadys. Explain what is
     meant by this, and translate the phrase into idiomatic English.   2
                                                                        ——
                                                                        25

18

Pliny, VII. 27.

Pliny tells Sura a story about the ghost of Africa, which leads him to believe in ghosts.

C. Plinius Surae suo S.
et mihi discendi et tibi docendi facultatem otium praebet. igitur **perquam** velim scire, 1
utrum esse **phantasmata** et habere propriam figuram numenque aliquod putes an inania
et vana ex metu nostro imaginem accipere. ego ut esse credam in primis eo ducor, quod
audio accidisse Curtio Rufo. **tenuis** adhuc et obscurus, **obtinenti** Africam comes haeserat.
inclinato die **spatiabatur** in porticu; offertur ei mulieris figura humana grandior 5
pulchriorque. perterrito Africam se futurorum praenuntiam dixit: iturum enim Romam
honoresque gesturum, atque etiam cum summo imperio in eandem provinciam
reversurum, ibique moriturum. facta sunt omnia. praeterea accedenti Carthaginem
egredientique nave eadem figura in litore occurrisse narratur. ipse certe **implicitus morbo**
futura praeteritis, adversa secundis auguratur, spem salutis nullo suorum desperante 10
proiecit.

Line	1	perquam	very much
	2	phantasma –atis (neut.)	ghost
	4	tenuis	unimportant
		obtinere	to be governor of
	5	spatiari	to stroll about
	9	implicari morbo	to fall ill

1. What Latin word does 'S' stand for in the greeting? 1
2. Why do Pliny and Sura have the chance to discuss ghosts? 1
3. Lines 1-3:
   (a) why is *velim* subjunctive? 1
   (b) what alternatives does Pliny see regarding ghosts? 5
4. What are the meanings here of *in primis* (3) and *quod* (3)? 2
5. When did the ghost appear? Describe its appearance. 1,3
6. What prediction does Africa make for Curtius? How do you know whether the prediction came true? 5,1
7. What was Curtius doing when Africa appeared a second time? 2
8. Explain what Pliny means by *futura praeteritis, adversa secundis auguratur* (10). 4
9. Why was Curtius' belief that he was going to die surprising? 1
10. Account for the cases of *comes* (4), *humana* (5), *accedenti* (8). 3

30

19

Livy, II. 13.

Porsenna, the Etruscan king, has been besieging Rome. When peace is concluded, the Romans give hostages, half of them girls.

Cloelia una ex obsidibus, cum castra Etruscorum forte haud procul a ripa Tiberis locata 1
essent, **frustrata** custodes, dux agminis virginum inter tela hostium Tiberim tranavit,
tutasque omnes Romam ad propinquos restituit. quod ubi regi nuntiatum est, primo
incensus ira oratores Romam misit ad Cloeliam poscendam; ceteras haud magni **facere.**
deinde in admirationem versus dixit si non dederetur obses, ruptum **foedus** se 5
existimaturum esse, sed, si dederetur, eam incolumem ad suos remissurum. **utrimque**
constitit fides; et Romani eam ex **foedere** restituerunt, et apud regem Etruscum non tuta
solum sed honorata virtus fuit, laudatamque virginem **parte** obsidum se **donare** dixit; ipsa
quos vellet legeret. pace **redintegrata** Romani novam in femina virtutem novo genere
honoris, statua equestri, **donaverunt**; in summa Sacra Via posita est virgo insidens equo. 10

Line	2	frustrari	a deponent verb
	4	facere	(here) to value
	5 & 7	foedus –eris (neut.)	treaty
	6	utrimque	on both sides
	8	pars partis	(here) half
	8 & 10	donare + acc. + abl.	to present somebody with something
	9	redintegrare	to renew

1. Where was the Etruscan camp?   1
2. What does Cloelia do in the first sentence (to *restituit*)?   5
3. Who are *omnes* (3)?   1
4. Explain the use and meaning of *quod* (3).   2
5. What was the king's first reaction to the news?   1
6. Translate *ad Cloeliam poscendam* (4). What is the perfect of *posco*?   2
7. What case is *magni* (4), and why is it in this case?   2
8. Why is *facere* (4) infinitive?   1
9. What are the king's second feelings about Cloelia's exploit?   1
10. What message does he now send to the Romans?   5
11. Say in your own words what, in the light of the rest of the sentence, *utrimque*
    constitit fides must mean (6).   2
12. How did the Romans react to the king's message (7)?   1
13. What does *ex* mean here (7)?   1
14. Lines 8-9: express in your own words all that Porsenna said to Cloelia.   5
15. Account for the subjunctives *vellet* and *legeret* (9).   2
16. Explain what is meant by *novam in femina virtutem* (9).   2
17. What form did the "equestrian statue" take?   1
                                                                                    ‾‾
                                                                                    35

How Verres, the unscrupulous governor of Sicily, acquired a most beautiful lampstand.

cum Antiochus, rex Syriae, candelabrum Romam afferret, ut in Capitolio poneret, 1
pervenit **res** ad Verris aures. ille igitur petit a rege ut id ad se mittat; dicit se cupere
inspicere. Antiochus, nihil de Verris **improbitate suspicatus**, suis imperat ut id in
praetorium quam occultissime deferrent. quo postquam attulerunt, ille splendore eius et
pulchritudine adeo attonitus est ut clamaret dignum esse regis dono, dignum Capitolio. 5
cum satis iam perspexisse videretur tollere incipiunt, sed dicit ille se velle id etiam magis
considerare; illos discedere iussit et candelabrum relinquere. rex primo nihil timebat,
nihil **suspicabatur**; dies unus, alter, plures; candelabrum non relatum est. rex nuntium
mittit ut id reddat; nihil relatum; tum ipse hominem **appellat** et rogat ut reddat. Verres
orare coepit ut id sibi daret, tandem minari. denique regem de provincia iubet ante 10
noctem decedere; se cognovisse ex eius regno piratas ad Siciliam esse venturos.

Line	2	res	the matter, fact
	3	improbitas –tatis	dishonesty
	3 & 8	suspicari is deponent	
	4	praetorium –ii	governor's residence
	9	appellare	to appeal to

1. Why was Antiochus bringing the lampstand to Rome? 1
2. Lines 2-3: what request does Verres make, and what reason does he give for the request? 2,2
3. What does Antiochus tell his men to do? 3
4. What does *quo* mean in line 4? 1
5. Explain what Verres means by *dignum esse regis dono, dignum Capitolio* (5). What case is *dono*? 3,1
6. Why did Antiochus's men start to take the lampstand away? 2
7. To whom or to what do these pronouns refer: *eius* (4), *ille* (6), *illos* (7)? 3
8. Translate *dies unus, alter, plures* (8) into idiomatic English, inserting an appropriate verb. 3
9. How does Antiochus first try to get the lampstand back? 2
10. What does Verres finally do to ensure that he keeps the lampstand himself, and what is his excuse? 2,3
11. What are the meanings of *de* in lines 3 and 10? 2
12. Identify the uses of *ut* in lines 1, 2 and 5? 3
13. Line 1. *afferret*: quote from the passage the perfect and past participle of *fero* in this or another compound? 2
  —
  35

Curtius, VII. ii. 19-27

Philotas, son of Parmenio, has been accused of treason against Alexander and executed; Parmenio does not know this. Parmenio is also accused, but is governor of Media, and Alexander has sent Polydamas with letters to Cleander and the other generals with Parmenio, telling them to kill him. Polydamas' excuse for visiting Parmenio is that he has letters for him from Alexander and Philotas.

priusquam ipsius nuntiaretur adventus, Polydamas in tabernaculum Cleandri quarta   1
vigilia pervenit. redditis deinde litteris, constituerunt prima luce ad Parmenionem coire.
iamque ceteris quoque ducibus litteras regis attulerat, iam ad eum venturi erant, cum
Parmenioni **Polydamanta** venisse nuntiaverunt. qui dum laetatur adventu amici, simulque
noscendi quae rex ageret avidus, **Polydamanta** requiri iubet.   5
   spatiabatur in nemore Parmenio, medius inter duces quibus erat imperatum ut
occiderent. agendae autem rei constituerant tempus, cum Parmenio litteras a
Polydamante traditas legere coepisset. Polydamas procul veniens, ut a Parmenione
conspectus est, vultu laetitiae speciem praeferente, ad complectendum eum cucurrit,
mutuaque salutatione facta, Polydamas epistulam a rege scriptam ei tradidit. Parmenio   10
vinculum epistulae solvens, quidnam rex ageret requirebat. ille ex ipsis litteris
cogniturum esse respondit. quibus Parmenio lectis: 'rex', inquit, 'expeditionem parat in
Arachosios. strenuum hominem et numquam cessantem! sed tempus saluti suae, tanta
iam **parta** gloria, parcere.' alteram deinde epistulam Philotae nomine scriptam laetus,
quod ex vultu notari poterat, legebat; tum eius latus gladio haurit Cleander, deinde   15
iugulum ferit, ceteri exanimum quoque confodiunt.

Line	4 & 5	Polydamas acc. Polydamanta	
	6	spatiari	to stroll
	13	parere partum	to gain

1. Lines 1-2:
    (a) at what time in modern terms did Polydamas reach Cleander?   1
    (b) what difference does it make to the meaning that Curtius wrote *nuntiaretur*
    rather than *nuntiatus est*?   2
2. Why is *nuntiaverunt* (4) indicative?   1
3. Why did Parmenio send men to look for Polydamas?   3
4. (a) When were the generals going to kill Parmenio?   2
    (b) Account for the mood and tense of *coepisset* (8).   2
5. How did Polydamas hide the true purpose of his visit when he met Parmenio?   2
6. What answer does the letter give to the question asked in line 11?   2
7. Line 13: account for the cases of *hominem* and *saluti*.   2
8. What is the point of *epistulam Philotae nomine scriptam* (14)?   2
9. Explain the use of *quod* (15).   1
10. Describe the actual execution of Parmenio.   4
11. Comment on Curtius' use of tenses with particular reference to *venturi erant*
    (3), *laetatur* (4), *spatiabatur* (6), *tradidit* (10), *legebat* (15), *haurit* (15).   6
                                                                                        ─────
                                                                                        30

317 BC Alexander the Great is dead, and his generals are battling for supremacy. Antigonus has control of the Asian part of Alexander's empire, but is being challenged by Eumenes who fights in the cause of Alexander's six year old son.
Part 1: *Antigonus tries to launch a surprise attack on Eumenes, but his own men give the game away.*

duae erant viae qua Antigonus ad adversariorum hibernas posset pervenire. quarum 1
brevior per loca deserta, quae nemo incolebat propter aquae inopiam, ceterum dierum
erat fere decem; illa autem, qua omnes **commeabant**, altero tanto longiorem habebat
anfractum sed erat copiosa omniumque rerum abundans. hac si proficisceretur,
Antigonus intellegebat prius adversarios cognituros de suo adventu quam ipse tertiam 5
partem confecisset itineris; sin per loca sola contenderet, sperabat se imprudentem
hostem oppressurum. ad hanc rem conficiendam imperavit cibum coctum dierum decem
comparari, ut quam minime fieret ignis in castris. sic paratus, qua constituerat
proficiscitur.
      dimidium fere spatium confecerat, cum ex **fumo** castrorum eius suspicio adlata 10
est ad Eumenem hostem appropinquare. conveniunt duces; quaeritur quid opus sit facto;
intellegebant omnes tam celeriter copias ipsorum contrahi non posse quam Antigonus
adfuturus videbatur. hic, omnibus desperantibus, Eumenes ait, si celeritatem vellent
adhibere, se effecturum ut non minus decem diebus hostis retardaretur; qua re
circumirent, suas quisque contraheret copias. 15

Line	3	commeare	to travel
	4	anfractus –us	roundabout route
	10	dimidium –ii	half
		fumus	the soldiers lit fires against the cold

1.	At what time of the year does this take place?	1
2.	In lines 1-7 what are the advantages and disadvantages of each route?	8
3.	Line 2: what is the meaning of *loca* as a neuter plural?	1
4.	*sic paratus* (8): what has Antigonus prepared, and what is its purpose?	3
5.	How does Nepos bring a sense of urgency and drama to lines 11-13?	2
6.	Translate *quaeritur quid opus sit facto*.	2
7.	What undertaking does Eumenes give the other generals?	3
8.	Account for the cases of *dierum* (2) and *diebus* (14).	2
9.	What are the meanings of *ceterum* (2) and *qua re* (14)?	2
10.	Explain the uses of *quam* in lines 5, 8 and 12.	3
11.	Account for the moods of *posset* (1), *adlata est* (10-11), *circumirent* (15).	3
		30

Nepos, *Eumenes* XVIII 9-10.

Part 2: *How Eumenes outwits Antigonus and delays his attack.*

ad Antigoni autem morandum impetum Eumenes tale capit consilium. certos mittit 1
homines ad infimos montes, qui obvii erant itineri adversariorum, iisque praecipit ut
prima nocte quam latissime ignes faciant quam maximos atque hos secunda vigilia
minuant, tertia perexiguos reddant et, simulata castrorum consuetudine, suspicionem
iniciant hostibus iis locis esse castra ac de eorum adventu esse praenuntiatum; idemque 5
postera nocte faciant. quibus imperatum erat diligenter praeceptum curant. Antigonus sub
vesperum ignes conspicatur; credit de suo adventu esse auditum et adversarios illuc suas
contraxisse copias. mutat consilium et, quoniam imprudentes adoriri non posset, flectit
iter suum et illum **anfractum** longiorem copiosae viae capit, ibique diem unum moratur
ad lassitudinem militum **sedandam** ac reficiendos equos, quo integriore exercitu 10
decerneret. sic Eumenes callidum imperatorem vicit consilio celeritatemque eius impedivit.

Line	9	anfractus –us	roundabout route
	10	sedare	to relieve

1. Why did Eumenes choose the mountains as the place to position his men?   2
2. Explain the basic intention of Eumenes' plan, and how the men are to achieve this.   2,4
3. What did Antigonus assume on seeing the fires?   2
4. Why in line 8 does Antigonus change his plan?   2
5. Why did Antigonus wait there for one day?   4
6. Which is the most emphatic word in the final sentence, and how does Nepos make it the most emphatic?   2
7. Explain with examples from this passage the impersonal uses of the passive.   4
8. What do these phrases mean here: *ad infimos montes* (2), *quam latissime* (3), *sub vesperum* (6-7)?   3
     25

Curio is Caesar's general in Africa, Varus Pompey's. Curio's men are enjoying a remarkably one-sided victory over Varus.
Part 1: *The rout and exemplary courage of Fabius.*

sed praeoccupatus animus Vari militum timore et fuga et caede suorum nihil de   1
resistendo cogitabat, omnesque iam se ab equitatu circumveniri arbitrabantur. itaque
prius quam telum adigi posset aut nostri propius accederent, omnis Vari acies terga vertit
seque in castra recepit.

    qua in fuga Fabius quidam ex infimis ordinibus de exercitu Curionis primum   5
agmen fugientium consecutus, magna voce Varum nomine appellans requirebat, uti unus
esse ex eius militibus et monere aliquid velle ac dicere videretur. ubi ille saepius
appellatus aspexit ac restitit et quis esset aut quid vellet quaesivit, umerum apertum
gladio appetit paulumque afuit quin Varum interficeret; quod ille periculum sublato scuto
vitavit. Fabius a proximis militibus circumventus interficitur.   10

1.	What are the thoughts of Varus' soldiers in lines 1-2?	4
2.	What were the results of these thoughts? Account for the subjunctives in line 3.	4,1
3.	What are we told about Fabius which makes his exploit the more remarkable?	2
4.	What part of Varus' army does he reach?	1
5.	What is Fabius saying as he goes, and why is he saying this?	1,3
6.	What does *saepius* (7) mean in this context? What does Varus say to Fabius?	1,2
7.	Where did Fabius try to hit Varus, and how did Varus save himself? Which one would have been *apertus*?	3
8.	Translate *paulum afuit quin Varum interficeret* (9).	2
9.	What happened to Fabius?	1
		25

Caesar, *De Bello Civili* II. 35

Part 2: *Curio's men pursue Varus and his men to their camp, but can not take it.*

hac fugientium multitudine et turba portae castrorum occupantur atque iter impeditur, 1
pluresque in eo loco sine vulnere quam in proelio aut fuga intereunt, neque multum afuit
quin etiam castris expellerentur. sed cum loci natura et munitio castrorum aditum
prohibebat, tum quod ad proelium egressi Curionis milites eis rebus **indigebant** quae ad
oppugnationem castrorum erant usui. itaque Curio exercitum reducit suis omnibus 5
praeter **Fabium** incolumibus, ex numero adversariorum circiter DC interfectis ac M
vulneratis; qui omnes discessu Curionis multique praeterea per simulationem vulnerum ex
castris in **oppidum** propter timorem sese recipiunt. qua re animadversa Varus et terrore
exercitus cognito **bucinatore** in castris et paucis ad speciem tabernaculis relictis de tertia
vigilia silentio exercitum in oppidum reducit. 10

Line 4	indigere + abl.	to lack
6	Fabius	this is the Fabius of Part 1 (p. 25)
8	oppidum	Varus held the nearby town of Utica
9	bucinator –ris	trumpeter

1. Why were the entrances of the camp blocked?   1
2. Line 1: *multitudine et turba* is an hendiadys. Explain what is meant by this 2
   and translate the phrase accordingly.
3. What were the results of the blocking of the entrances? 5
4. Lines 3-5: what saved the camp from being taken? Why is *cum* followed by
   an indicative? Account for the case of *usui*.   4,1,1
5. What casualties were suffered on the two sides? 3
6. What sign was there of the fear in Varus army? 2
7. How did Varus get the rest of the army into the town without being noticed?
   What is the meaning of *ad* here?   4,1
8. At one point Caesar, as he often does, has omitted part of *esse*. Where?   1
                                                      25

490 BC Darius, king of Persia, plans to invade Greece. After capturing Eretria, his generals land at Marathon, and the Athenians have to decide how to deal with them.

Darius autem, hortantibus amicis ut Graeciam vinceret, classem quingentarum navium 1
comparavit, eique **Datim** praefecit et **Artaphernen**, eisque ducenta peditum, decem milia
equitum dedit. illi, ubi ad **Euboeam** navigaverunt, celeriter Eretriam ceperunt omnesque
eius oppidi cives abreptos in Asiam ad regem miserunt. inde ad **Atticam** accesserunt ac
suas copias in campum **Marathona** deduxerunt.   5
    hoc tumultu tam propinquo territi Athenienses Phidippidem **Lacedaemonem**
miserunt ut a Lacedaemoniis peteret ut auxilium celeriter mitterent. ipsi deliberabant
utrum moenibus se defenderent an egressi hostibus acie resisterent. at Miltiades, dux
Atheniensium, maxime eos hortabatur ut quam primum copias educeret; putabat enim et
cives fortiores futuros esse, cum viderent se de eorum virtute non desperare, et hostes 10
cautiores, si conspicerent Athenienses audere contra se tam parvis copiis pugnare.

Line	2	Datis acc. Datim	
		Artaphernes acc. Artaphernen	
	3	Euboea –ae	Euboea, an island off the east coast of Greece
	4	Attica –ae	Attica, region of Greece of which Athens was capital
	5	Marathon acc. Marathona	
	6	Lacedaemon –nis	the city of Sparta

1.   What was the advice of Darius' friends?   1
2.   What forces did Datis and Artaphernes have under their command?   3
3.   What did Datis and Artaphernes do with the citizens of Eretria?   3
4.   Line 6, *territi*: why were the Athenians terrified?   2
5.   Identify the uses of *ut* in line 7.   2
6.   What were the Athenians discussing in lines 7-8?   5
7.   What was Miltiades's view?   2
8.   Explain his reasoning behind this preference.   7
9.   Give the 1st person of the present of the simple verbs of which *abreptos* (4)
      and *accesserunt* (4) are compounds.   2
10.   Account for the subjunctives *defenderent* (8) and *conspicerent* (11).   2,1
11.   Account for the cases of *amicis* (1), *ei* (2), *equitum* (3), *hostibus* (8) and
      hostes (10).   <u>5</u>
                                                       35

Cicero, *De Officiis* I. 39. xiii.

Individuals must keep promises, even if made to enemies and under duress.

atque etiam si quid singuli temporibus adducti hosti promiserunt, est in eo ipso fides 1
conservanda, ut primo Punico bello Regulus captus a Poenis cum de captivis
commutandis Romam missus esset iurassetque se rediturum, primum, ut venit, captivos
reddendos in senatu non censuit, deinde, cum retineretur a propinquis et ab amicis, ad
supplicium redire maluit quam fidem hosti datam fallere. 5

Line 5	supplicium	torture and death

1. What Latin words correspond to "must keep promises" and "under duress"? 2
2. (a) Which Latin verbs are dependent on *ut* (2)? 2
   (b) What are the meanings of *ut* in lines 2 and 3? 2
3. Why was Regulus sent to Rome, and what was surprising about the opinion which he gave in the Senate? 1,2
4. Comment on the form of *iurasset* (3). 1
5. Give the present indicative 1st person singular of the verbs of which *rediturum* (3) and *reddendos* (4) are parts. 2
6. What is the meaning of *cum* in line 4? 1
7. (a) Translate lines 4-5 (*ad supplicium* to *fallere*). 3
   (b) Quote from the passage the Latin words of his promise. 1
8. Compare the meanings in relation to their cases of the gerundives *conservanda* (2), *commutandis* (3), and *reddendos* (4). 3

20

Caesar, *De Bello Gallico* III. 11.

Caesar's dispositions of his forces in Gaul.

itaque T. Labienum legatum in Treveros, qui proximi flumini Rheno sunt, cum equitatu 1
mittit. huic mandat, Remos reliquosque Belgas adeat atque **in officio contineat**,
Germanosque, qui auxilio a Belgis arcessiti dicebantur, si per vim navibus flumen
transire conentur, prohibeat. P. Crassum cum cohortibus legionariis xii et magno numero
equitatus in Aquitaniam proficisci iubet, ne ex his nationibus auxilia in Galliam mittantur 5
ac tantae nationes coniungantur. Q. Titurium Sabinum legatum cum legionibus tribus in
Venellos, Curiosolitas Lexoviosque mittit, qui eam manum **distinendam** curet. D. Brutum
adulescentem classi Gallicisque navibus, quas ex Pictonibus et Santonis reliquisque
pacatis regionibus convenire iusserat, praeficit et cum primum posset in Venetos
proficisci iubet. ipse eo pedestribus copiis contendit.   10

Line 2	in officio continere	to keep (somebody) loyal
7	distinere	to keep apart

1. Where did the Treveri live?   1
2. What instructions did Caesar give to Labienus?   4
3. Explain why *dicebantur* (3) is indicative, but *conentur* (4) subjunctive.   2
4. Why was Crassus sent to Aquitania?   2
5. Translate line 7 *qui* to *curet*.   2
6. What orders did Caesar give to Brutus?   2
7. What are the cases of *auxilio* (3) and *Gallicis navibus* (8), and why are they in   2
    these cases?
8. Account for the tense and mood of *posset* (9).   2
9. What is the meaning here of *eo* (10)?   1
10. Roughly how many men would there have been in:
    (a) cohortibus legionariis xii (4),
    (b) *legionibus tribus* (6)?   2
                                                                                                  ――
                                                                                                  20

BC 112. Adherbal shares the rule of the kingdom of Numidia with his brother Hiempsal and his cousin Jugurtha; but Jugurtha does not want to have to share. Cirta was the capital of Numidia.

Adherbal ubi intellegit **eo processum uti** regnum aut relinquendum esset aut armis 1
retinendum, necessario copias parat et Jugurthae obvius procedit. interim haud longe a
mari prope Cirtam oppidum utriusque exercitus consedit, et, quia diei extremum erat,
proelium non inceptum. sed ubi plerumque noctis processit, obscuro etiam tum lumine,
milites Jugurthini signo dato castra hostium invadunt; semisomnos partim, alios arma 5
sumentes fugant funduntque.
Adherbal cum paucis equitibus Cirtam profugit, et, ni multitudo **togatorum**
fuisset, quae Numidas insequentes moenibus prohibuit, uno die inter duos reges coeptum
atque **patratum** bellum foret. igitur Jugurtha oppidum circumsedit, vineis turribusque et
machinis omnium generum expugnare aggreditur. Italici, quorum virtute moenia 10
defensabantur, confisi, deditione facta, propter magnitudinem populi Romani inviolatos
sese fore, Adherbali suadent uti seque et oppidum Jugurthae tradat, tantum ab eo vitam
paciscatur; de ceteris senatui curae fore.

Line	1	eo processum uti	things had reached the point that ...
	7	togati –orum	Roman citizens
	9	patrare	to finish
	13	pacisci + ab + acc.	to bargain with ... for ...

1. What choice does Adherbal face in lines 1-2?   2
2. Where will the battle be fought? Why is it not fought at once?   2
3. When does the fighting start, and what is the first move in it?   2
4. Why do Jugurtha's men meet so little resistance?   2
5. What prevented Jugurtha's immediate capture of Cirta?   1
6. Why were the Romans not frightened by the prospect of the city's surrender?   3
7. What advice did they give Adherbal?   4
8. Account for the cases of *Jugurthae* (2) and *curae* (13).   2
9. Explain the syntax of *proelium inceptum* (4).   1
10. What parts of what verbs are *foret* (9), *confisi* (11), *fore* (13)?   3
11. Give the meanings of these words: *utriusque* (3), *quia* (3), *fugant* (6).   <u>3</u>
    25

Some men may sacrifice everything for their country, except their own honour.
During the Peloponnesian War (431-404 BC) the Spartans (Lacedaemonii) were
heavily defeated by the Athenians in 406 off the Arginusae Islands.

inventi autem multi sunt, qui non modo pecuniam, sed etiam vitam profundere pro patria 1
parati essent, iidem gloriae **iacturam** ne minimam quidem facere vellent, ne republica
quidem postulante; ut Callicratidas, qui, cum Lacedaemoniorum dux fuisset
Peloponnesiaco bello multaque fecisset egregie, **vertit** ad extremum omnia, cum consilio
non paruit eorum, qui classem ab Arginusis removendam nec cum Atheniensibus 5
dimicandum putabant; quibus ille respondit Lacedaemonios classe illa amissa aliam
parare posse, se fugere sine suo dedecore non posse.

Line	2	iactura –ae	loss
	4	vertere (here)	to destroy, ruin
	6	dimicare	to fight

1. What contrast is Cicero making in lines 1-3, and how does he emphasise the
   contrast?   4,2
2. Why is *essent* (2) subjunctive?   1
3. What is the meaning of *ut* in line 3?   1
4. What is unusual about the word order in line 4 (*multa ... omnia*)? Show what
   effect Cicero achieves by this word order.   2,2
5. Why is *cum* used with a subjunctive in lines 3-4, but with an indicative later
   in lines 4-5?   2
6. What advice was Callicratidas given?   2
7. Quote and translate the Latin words which tell you whether he took this
   advice.   2
8. Compare the constructions and meanings of *removendam* (5) and
   dimicandum (6).   4
9. Express in idiomatic English in direct speech Callicratidas's answer to his
   advisers (lines 6-7).   4
10. How does Cicero use sound and word order in lines 6-7 to point the contrast
    and make the lines more emphatic?   <u>4</u>
                 30

Curtius, IV. ii. 10-16.

332 BC Alexander has been refused admission to the city of Tyre by its citizens. Tyre stood on an island, about half a mile from the mainland.

inter quae parva res Tyriorum fiduciam accendit. Carthaginiensium legati ad   1
celebrandum sacrum anniversarium more patrio tunc venerant; quippe Carthaginem Tyrii
condiderunt, semper parentum loco culti. hortari ergo Poeni coeperunt ut obsidionem
forti animo paterentur; brevi Carthagine auxilia ventura.

    Alexander autem, cum et classem procul haberet et longam obsidionem magno   5
sibi **ad cetera** impedimento videret fore, **caduceatores** qui ad pacem eos compellerent
misit; quos Tyrii contra ius gentium occisos praecipitaverunt in altum. atque ille, suorum
tam indigna morte commotus, urbem obsidere statuit.

    sed ante iacienda moles erat quae continenti urbem coniungeret. ingens ergo
animis militum desperatio incessit cernentibus profundum mare, quod vix divina ope   10
posset impleri; quae saxa tam vasta, quas tam **proceras** arbores posse reperiri?

Line 6	ad cetera	'with regard to the rest of his campaign'
6	caduceator –ris	envoy with a flag of truce
11	procerus –a –um	high, lofty

1.   Why did the Carthaginians celebrate an annual festival in Tyre?   2
2.   How did their arrival give confidence to the Tyrians?   3
3.   (a) What were Alexander's reasons for sending envoys to Tyre, and what   4
    were the envoys to do?
    (b) Why is *compellerent* (6) subjunctive?   1
4.   (a) What did the Tyrians do to the envoys?   2
    (b) What is *ius gentium* in modern terms?   1
5.   What part of speech is *ante* in line 9?   1
6.   (a) What was the mood of the soldiers?   1
    (b) Why did they feel this way?   3
    (c) What appears to be illogical about the case of *cernentibus*?   2
7.   In line 11 explain why *posset* is subjunctive, and *posse* infinitive.   2
8.   Account for the cases of *brevi* (4), *Carthagine* (4), *impedimento* (6).   3
                                                                   25

Caesar, *De Bello Gallico* III. 26.

The Gauls have fortified a camp in the Roman style. Crassus, the Roman general, has decided that he has to attack it. Cavalry have reported that the rear of the camp is less well fortified.

Crassus equitum praefectos cohortatus, ut magnis praemiis pollicitationibusque suos 1
excitarent, quid fieri velit ostendit. illi, ut erat imperatum, eductis eis cohortibus quae
praesidio castris relictae **intritae** ab labore erant, et longiore itinere circumductis, ne ex
hostium castris conspici possent, omnium oculis mentibusque ad pugnam intentis
celeriter ad **eas quas diximus munitiones** pervenerunt atque his **prorutis** prius in hostium 5
castris constiterunt quam plane ab eis videri aut quid rei gereretur cognosci posset. tum
vero clamore ab ea parte audito, nostri redintegratis viribus, quod plerumque in spe
victoriae accidere consuevit, acrius impugnare coeperunt. hostes undique circumventi,
desperatis omnibus rebus, se per munitiones deicere et fuga salutem petere intenderunt.
quos equitatus apertissimis campis consectatus ex milium L numero, quae ex Aquitania 10
Cantabrisque convenisse constabat, vix quarta parte relicta, multa nocte se in castra
recipit.

Line 3	intritus –a –um	not worn out
5	eas … munitiones	i.e. in the rear of the camp
	proruere	to overthrow, destroy

1. What does Crassus tell his cavalry commanders in the first sentence? — 3
2. Which cohorts do the cavalry commanders lead out in lines 2-3? — 2
3. Why do they take a roundabout route? — 2
4. Quote and translate the Latin words which tell you the mood of the soldiers. — 2
5. How does Caesar emphasise the speed with which the Romans arrived, destroyed the fortifications at the rear of the camp, and entered it? — 3
6. Translate *quod plerumque in spe victoriae accidere consuevit* (7-8). — 3
7. Why did the enemy abandon all hope? — 1
8. Why were the cavalry so successful in their pursuit? Roughly how many Gauls got away? — 1,1
9. Account for the cases of *rei* (6) and *quae* (10). — 2
10. Why are these verbs subjunctive: *gereretur* (6), *posset* (6)? — 2
11. What are the meanings of these words or phrases: *redintegratis viribus* (7), *constabat* (11), *multa nocte* (11)? — 3
  — 25

Livy, I. 56.

510 BC A terrible omen has occurred in the palace of Tarquinius Superbus, and he decides to consult the oracle at Delphi in Greece. He sends two of his three sons and his nephew, Brutus. The Delphic oracle was notorious for producing answers which were fulfilled in unexpected ways.

Tarquinius hoc visu exterritus Delphos ad maxime **inclitum** in terris oraculum mittere   1
statuit, neque responsa **sortium** ulli alii committere ausus, duos filios per ignotas eo
tempore terras, ignotiora maria in Graeciam misit. Titus et Arruns profecti; comes iis
additus Lucius Iunius Brutus. postquam Delphos ventum est, perfectis patris mandatis
cupido incessit animos iuvenum cognoscendi ad quem eorum regnum Romanum esset   5
venturum. ex infimo **specu** vocem redditam ferunt: 'imperium summum habebit qui
vestrum primus, o iuvenes, **osculum** matri tulerit.' Titus et Arruns ut Sextus, qui Romae
relictus fuerat, ignarus responsi **expersque** imperii esset, rem summa ope taceri iubent;
ipsi inter se uter prior, cum Romam redisset, matri osculum daret, **sorti** permittunt.
Brutus **alio** ratus **spectare** oraculi vocem, velut si prolapsus cecidisset, terram **osculo**   10
contigit, scilicet quod ea communis mater omnium mortalium esset. reditum inde
Romam.

Line	1	inclitus	famous
	2 & 9	sors sortis	oracle (2), drawing of lots (9)
	6	specus –us	cave
	7 & 10	osculum –i	kiss
	8	expers + gen..	having no share in
	10	alio spectare	to refer to something else

1. Why did Tarquinius choose Delphi as the oracle to consult?   2
2. How does Livy show that this was an unusual choice?   3
3. What was the first thing that the young men did on arriving in Delphi?   2
4. To what further question did they want an answer?   2
5. What answer did the oracle give? Account for the tense of *tulerit* (7).   3,1
6. Why did Titus and Arruns want this answer kept secret?   3
7. For what did they then draw lots?   2
8. What did Brutus do, and what was his reason for doing this?   3,2
9. Explain the syntax and meaning of *reditum* (11).   2
10. What are the meanings of *ferunt* (6), *velut* (10), *scilicet* (11)?   3
11. Give the present infinitives of *ausus* (2), *ratus* (10), *prolapsus* (10), *cecidisset* (10).   4
12. In what cases are *alii* (2), *cupido* (5), *vestrum* (7)?   3
                                                                    ___
                                                                    35

The unexpected fulfilment of this oracle came when Brutus became one of the first two consuls in Rome on the expulsion of Tarquinius.

478 BC Pausanias, who had commanded the Spartans in the memorable defeat of the Persians at Plataea in 479, now commands a Greek fleet sent to drive the Persians from Cyprus and the Hellespont, but treacherously conspires with Xerxes, the Persian king.

cum **Byzantio** expugnato complures Persarum nobiles cepisset atque in his nonnullos 1
regis propinquos, hos clam Xerxi remisit, simulans eos ex vinculis publicis effugisse, et
cum his Gongylum qui litteras regi redderet, in quibus haec sunt scripta: 'Pausanias, dux
Spartae, quos Byzanti ceperat, postquam propinquos tuos cognovit, tibi muneri misit,
seque tecum **adfinitate** coniungi cupit; qua re, si tibi videtur, des ei filiam tuam nuptum. 5
id si feceris, et Spartam et ceteram Graeciam sub tuam potestatem se adiuvante te
redacturum pollicetur.'
    rex, magno opere gavisus, confestim cum epistula Artabazum ad Pausaniam
mittit, in qua petit ne cui rei parcat ad ea efficienda quae pollicetur; si perfecerit, nullius rei
a se **repulsam** laturum. huius Pausanias voluntate cognita, alacrior ad rem gerendam factus, 10
in suspicionem cecidit **Lacedaemoniorum**. quo facto domum revocatus. accusatus capitis
absolvitur, **multatur** tamen pecunia; quam ob causam ad classem remissus non est.

Line	1	Byzantium –i	now Istanbul
	5	adfinitas –tatis	alliance by marriage
	10	repulsa –ae	refusal
	11	Lacedaemonii –orum	Spartans
	12	multare	to punish

1.	What important prisoners did Pausanias capture in Byzantium?	2
2.	What did he pretend happened to them?	2
3.	(a) What offer does Pausanias make to Xerxes in lines 5-7?	3
	(b) What does *si tibi videtur* (5) mean in idiomatic English?	2
	(c) Explain the syntax of *nuptum* (5).	2
4.	Quote and translate the words which describe Xerxes' reaction to the letter.	2
5.	Translate *petit ne cui rei parcat ad ea efficienda quae pollicetur* (9) into idiomatic English.	3
6.	What promise does Xerxes make in line 9-10?	2
7.	What was the judgement in Pausanias' trial?	2
8.	Quote from the passage another phrase with the same meaning as *quam ob causam* (12).	1
9.	Account for the subjunctives *redderet* (3) and *des* (5).	2
10.	Account for the cases of *muneri* (4) and *capitis* (12).	2
		25

330 BC After twice being heavily defeated by Alexander, Darius was deposed by his own followers, and then hunted down and killed. Alexander is now recognised as King of Persia, as well as Macedonia, and has leading Persians among his bodyguard. A Persian, Spitamenes, now brings him Bessus, who killed Darius.

Spitamenes eum tenebat collo inserta catena, tam barbaris quam Macedonibus gratum   1
spectaculum. tum Spitamenes: 'et te', inquit, 'et Dareum, reges meos, ultus,
interfectorem domini sui adduxi, eo modo captum, cuius ipse fecit exemplum. aperiat ad
hoc spectaculum oculos Dareus! **exsistat ab inferis**, qui illo **supplicio** indignus fuit et
hoc solacio dignus est!'   5
    Alexander, multum collaudato Spitamene, Oxathren, fratrem Darei, quem inter
corporis custodes habebat, propius accedere iussit, tradique Bessum ei, ut cruci affixum,
mutilatis auribus naribusque, sagittis configerent barbari asservarentque corpus, ut ne
aves quidem contigerent. Oxathres cetera sibi curae fore pollicetur; aves non ab alio
quam a Catane posse prohiberi adicit, **eximiam** eius artem cupiens ostendere; namque   10
adeo certo ictu **destinata** feriebat, ut aves quoque exciperet. nunc forsitan, sagittarum
celebri usu, minus admirabilis videri ars haec possit; tum ingens visentibus miraculum
magnoque honori Catani fuit. dona deinde omnibus qui Bessum adduxerant data sunt.
ceterum **supplicium** eius distulit, ut eo loco ipso, quo Dareum ipse occiderat, necaretur.   14

Line	4	exsistere ab inferis	to rise from the dead
	4 & 14	supplicium –i	fate, death
	10	eximius –a –um	exceptional
	11	destinatum –i	mark, target
	12	celeber –bris (gen.) –bre (neut. nom.)	frequent, regular

1. In lines 1-5:
    (a) How do the Persians and Macedonians regard the capture of Bessus, and how would Darius feel about it?   2
    (b) What does Spitamenes feel is appropriate about the capture?   2
    (c) Why is *aperiat* (3) subjunctive?   1
2. What does Alexander order to be done with Bessus?   5
3. What promise does Oxathres make?   2
4. Why does Oxathres regard Catanes as the only proper person to guard the body?   3
5. What change does Curtius say there has been between "then" and "now"?   3
6. Why did Alexander delay the execution of Bessus?   2
7. Account for the cases of *supplicio* (4), *curae* (9), *visentibus* (12), *honori* (13).   4
8. What do these words mean: *tam ... quam ...* (1), *forsitan* (11), *ceterum* (14)?   3
9. Give the present infinitives of these verbs: *ultus* (2), *feriebat* (11), *distulit* (14).   3
                                                                                         ——
                                                                                         30

Cato answers the complaint that memory and mental faculties fail in old age. Sophocles, the Athenian writer of tragedies, composed 'Oedipus at Colonus' when he was ninety in 406 BC. It was first performed in 401, five years after his death.

at memoria minuitur. credo, nisi eam exerceas, aut si sis natura **tardior**. ego quidem non   1
modo eos **novi** qui sunt, sed eorum patres etiam et avos. nec **sepulcra legens** vereor, ut
dicunt, ne memoriam perdam; his ipsis legendis in memoriam redeo mortuorum. nec vero
quemquam senem audivi oblitum esse quo loco **thesaurum** celavisset. omnia quae curant
meminerunt; qui sibi, cui ipsi pecuniam debeant. manent **ingenia** senibus, **modo**   5
permaneat studium et industria.
    Sophocles ad summam senectutem tragoedias fecit; cum propter hoc studium **rem
familiarem** neglegere videretur, a filiis in iudicium vocatus est ut illum quasi **desipientem
a re familiari** removerent iudices. tum senex dicitur eam fabulam quam in manibus
habebat et proxime scripserat, Oedipum Coloneum, recitavisse iudicibus rogavisseque   10
num illud carmen **desipientis** videretur. quo recitato sententiis iudicum liberatus est.

Line 1	tardus	slow, stupid
2	novi	I know
	sepulcra legens	superstition said that reading tombstones damaged one's memory
4	thesaurus –i	buried treasure
5	ingenium –i	mental faculties
	modo + subj.	provided that
7 & 8, 9	res familiaris	family affairs and property
8 & 11	desipiens –tis	out of one's mind, foolish

1.   Under what circumstances does Cato accept that memory fails?   3
2.   Whom does Cato claim to know, and how does he know the latter pair?   3,1
3.   What are the uses of *ut* and *ne* in lines 2-3?   2
4.   What does Cato consider that nobody forgets, even when old?   4
5.   Why in line 6 is *permaneat* singular?   1
6.   Give an appropriate translation for *summam* (7) in this context.   1
7.   Why did Sophocles' sons take him to court, and what was their intention?   2,2
8.   What is the meaning of *quasi* (8)?   1
9.   How did Sophocles answer the charge? What Latin word tells you whether he won? Account for the case of *desipientis* (11).   5,1,1
10.   What would be an appropriate translation of *sententiis* (11)?   1
11.   Give the 1st person singular of the verbs used in the passage for "remember" and "forget".   2
                                                         30

Nepos, *Hannibal* XXIII. 10.

After the defeat of Carthage in the second Punic war, Hannibal stayed for a period in Carthage, but was then forced to flee. He continued his opposition to Rome, and in this story helps Prusias of Bithynia in his war against Eumenes of Pergamum.

Part 1

dissidebat ab eo Pergamenus rex Eumenes, Romanis amicissimus, bellumque inter eos   1
gerebatur et mari et terra; quo magis cupiebat eum Hannibal opprimi. sed utrobique
Eumenes plus valebat propter Romanorum societatem; quem si removisset, Hannibal
faciliora sibi cetera fore arbitrabatur. die ipso, quo facturus erat navale proelium, nautas
convocat iisque praecipit, omnes ut in unam Eumenis regis concurrant navem, a ceteris   5
tantum satis habeant se defendere; rex autem in qua nave veheretur, ut scirent, se
facturum; quem si aut cepissent aut interfecissent, magno iis pollicetur praemio fore.

Line 1	dissidere ab	to be opposed to

1. Why was Hannibal all the more keen for Eumenes to be defeated?   1
2. Line 2. What is the force of the suffix *-que* on *utrobique*? Explain the meaning
    of *utrobique* here. Translate *plus valebat* (3).   1,2,1
3. What did Hannibal think would be the result if he got rid of Eumenes?   2
4. What orders did Hannibal give the sailors before the battle?   4
5. What is unusual about the word order of line 5 (*omnes ... navem*), and what is
    its effect?   3
6. Translate lines 6-7, *rex* to *facturum.*   4
7. Account for the cases of *quo* (4) and *praemio* (7).   2
8. Why are these verbs in the subjunctive: *habeant* (6), *veheretur* (6), *cepissent* (7)?   3
9. What parts of the verb are *opprimi* (2), *fore* (7)?   2
                                                                                          ──
                                                                                          25

Part 2

tali cohortatione militum facta classis ab utrisque in proelium deducitur. quarum acie 1
constituta, priusquam signum pugnae daretur, Hannibal, ut palam faceret suis quo loco
Eumenes esset, **tabellarium** in **scapha** cum **caduceo** mittit. qui ubi ad naves adversariorum
pervenit epistulamque ostendens se regem professus est quaerere, statim ad Eumenem
deductus est, quod nemo dubitabat quin aliquid de pace esset scriptum. **tabellarius** nave 5
ducis suis declarata eodem, unde erat egressus, se recepit. at Eumenes soluta epistula
nihil in ea repperit nisi quae **ad** irridendum eum **pertinerent**. cuius etsi causam mirabatur
neque reperiebat, tamen proelium statim committere non dubitavit. horum in concursu
Bithynii Hannibalis praecepto universi navem Eumenis adoriuntur. quorum vim rex cum
sustinere non posset, fuga salutem petit, quam consecutus non esset, nisi intra sua 10
praesidia se recepisset, quae in proximo litore erant collocata.

Line 3 & 5	tabellarius	courier
	scapha	small boat
	caduceus	herald's staff (like a white flag of truce)
7	pertinere ad	to be aimed at, intended to

1. Line 1 *quarum*: account for its gender and number. 2
2. Why did Hannibal send the courier? 2
3. When he reached the enemy fleet, what did the courier say? 2
4. Why was the courier immediately taken to Eumenes? 3
5. What is the meaning of *eodem* (6)? 1
6. What did Eumenes find that the letter contained? 3
7. What is the antecedent of *cuius* (7)? 1
8. What were Eumenes' feelings on reading the letter? 1
9. Translate lines 9-11, *quorum* to *recepisset*, into idiomatic English. 5
10. Compare the meanings of *dubito* in lines 5 and 8, and the constructions
    dependent on the verb. 2
11. Why are the following verbs subjunctive: *daretur* (2), *esset* (3), *pertinerent* (7)? 3
    —
    25

Caesar, *De Bello Civili* III. 47.

48 BC Pompey has made Dyrrachium (now Durazzo or Durrës in Albania) his base for operations. Caesar attempts an unusual – and ultimately unsuccessful – form of siege when Pompey camps on a nearby hill.

erat nova belli ratio cum tot castellorum numero tantoque spatio et tantis munitionibus et   1
toto obsidionis genere, tum etiam reliquis rebus. nam quicumque alterum obsidere conati
sunt, perculsos atque infirmos hostes adorti aut proelio superatos aut aliqua **offensione**
permotos continuerunt, cum ipsi numero equitum militumque praestarent; causa autem
obsidionis haec fere esse consuevit, ut frumento hostes prohiberent. at tum integras atque   5
incolumes copias Caesar inferiore militum numero continebat, cum illi omnium rerum
copia abundarent; cotidie enim magnus undique navium numerus conveniebat quae
commeatum supportarent, neque ullus flare ventus poterat quin aliqua ex parte secundum
cursum haberent. ipse autem consumptis omnibus longe lateque frumentis summis erat in
angustiis. sed tamen haec singulari patientia milites ferebant. recordabantur enim eadem   10
se superiore anno in Hispania perpessos labore et patientia maximum bellum confecisse.

Line 3	offensio –onis	setback

1. (a) In what respects was this an unusual form of warfare?   4
    (b) What is the meaning of *cum ... tum* (1-2)?   1
2. Lines 2-5: what have usually been the circumstances of a siege?   5
3. In what ways are the circumstances now different?   3
4. (a) Why is there a *copia omnium rerum* (6-7)?   4
    (b) Why is *supportarent* (8) subjunctive?   1
    (c) Explain the use of *quin* in line 8?   2
5. In lines 9-10 how does Caesar's position differ from Pompey's?   2
6. What helps Caesar's men to endure their sufferings?   2
7. What would be appropriate idiomatic translations in their contexts of
    permotos (4), *consuevit* (5), *cum* (6), *parte* (8).   4
8. What are the meanings of the suffixes *-cumque* and *-que*, as in *quicumque* (2)
    and *undique* (7)?   2
                                                                                      _____
                                                                                          30

Pliny, I. 12. 9-13

For thirty five years Corellius has suffered an increasingly painful disease. Now he has committed suicide to be free of the pain, and Pliny writes to tell Calestrius of his grief at the death of their friend.

iam dies alter, tertius, quartus; abstinebat cibo. misit ad me uxor eius Hispulla 1
communem amicum C. Geminium cum tristissimo nuntio, destinasse Corellium mori,
nec aut suis aut filiae precibus inflecti; solum superesse me, a quo revocari posset ad
vitam. cucurri. perveneram in proximum cum mihi ab Hispulla Iulius Atticus nuntiat
nihil iam ne me quidem **impetraturum.** 5
      cogito quo amico, quo viro **caream.** implevit quidem annum septimum et
sexagensimum, quae aetas et robustissimis satis longa est; scio. evasit perpetuam
valetudinem; scio. decessit **superstitibus** suis, florente re publica, quae illi omnibus carior
erat; et hoc scio. ego tamen tamquam et iuvenis et firmissimi mortem doleo, doleo autem
(licet me **imbecillum** putes) **meo nomine.** amisi enim, amisi vitae meae **testem** rectorem 10
magistrum. proinde adhibe solacia mihi, non haec: 'senex erat, infirmus erat' (haec enim
novi), sed nova aliqua, sed magna, quae audierim numquam, legerim numquam. nam
quae audivi quae legi sponte **succurrunt**, sed tanto dolore superantur.

Line	5	impetrare	to achieve
	6	carere + abl.	to have lost
	8	superstes –titis	surviving
	10	imbecillus	weak, feeble
		meo nomine	on my own account, for my own sake
		testis –is	witness
	13	succurrere	to come to mind

1. How has Corellius decided to die?   1
2. What message does Geminius bring?   4
3. What news does Atticus bring? What do you observe about the negatives in this sentence?   2,1
4. In lines 6-9 what thoughts does Pliny cite to comfort himself in his loss?   5
5. In lines 9-11 Pliny describes the sort of grief he feels, and the reason he feels it; what are these?   2,2
6. Translate *licet me imbecillum putes* (10).   2
7. Why does Pliny want Calestrius to offer him words of comfort that he has never heard or read?   2
8. With close reference to the text show how in the second paragraph Pliny uses word order and other stylistic techniques to bring out the depth of his feelings.   5
9. Account for the moods of *nuntiat* (4) and *audierim* (12).   2
10. Account for the cases of *superstitibus* (8) and *omnibus* (8).   <u>2</u>
          30

Cicero, *In Verrem* II. iv. 54.120 – 55.122.

Cicero contrasts the treatment of Syracuse by Marcellus, who captured it in 211 BC, with that of Verres, who was a peace-time governor of Sicily, 73-70 BC. Insula was an island connected to Syracuse by a bridge.

Marcellus, cum tam praeclaram urbem vi copiisque cepisset, non putavit ad laudem populi Romani hoc **pertinere**, hanc puchritudinem, ex qua praesertim periculi nihil ostenderetur, delere et exstinguere. itaque aedificiis omnibus, publicis privatis, sacris profanis, sic pepercit quasi ad ea defendenda cum exercitu, non oppugnanda venisset. **conferte** Verrem, non ut hominem cum homine comparetis, sed ut pacem cum bello,   5 leges cum vi, forum et iuris **dicionem** cum ferro et armis **conferatis**.

    aedis Minervae est in Insula, quam Marcellus non attigit, quam plenam atque ornatam reliquit; quae ab isto sic spoliata atque direpta est, non ut ab hoste aliquo, sed ut a barbaris praedonibus vexata esse videatur. pugna erat equestris Agathocli regis in tabulis picta; iis autem tabulis interiores templi **parietes** vestiebantur. nihil erat ea pictura   10 nobilius, nihil **Syracusis**, quod magis visendum putaretur. has tabulas Marcellus, cum omnia victoria illa sua **profana** fecisset, tamen religione impeditus non attigit; iste, cum illa iam propter diuturnam pacem fidelitatemque populi Syracusani sacra religiosaque accepisset, omnes eas tabulas abstulit, **parietes**, quorum ornatus tot saecula manserant, tot bella effugerant, nudos ac deformatos reliquit.   15

Line	2	pertinere ad	to lead to
	5 & 6	conferre	to compare
	6	dicio –onis	rule
Line	10 & 14	paries –ietis	wall
	11	Syracusae –arum	Syracuse
	12	profanus –a –um	stripped of its religious protection

1. The first sentence gives two reasons why Marcellus did not destroy Syracuse. What are they?   4
2. Explain the contrast that Cicero makes between the behaviour of Marcellus and of Verres in lines 7-9. Show how lines 5-6 reinforce this contrast.   4,3
3. With what were the inside walls of Minerva's temple decorated?   2
4. How does Cicero emphasis the fame of this decoration?   2
5. Line 12: what is the meaning of *cum* here?   1
6. *omnia profana fecisset* (12): this contradicts something earlier on. What is the contradiction, and why has Cicero allowed it?   2,2
7. How does Cicero emphasise the barbarity of Verres' behaviour in lines 14-15?   4
8. Account for the cases of *periculi* (2), *pictura* (10), *Syracusis* (11).   3
9. Give the present infinitives and their meanings of *pepercit* (4), *attigit* (12), *abstulit* (14).   3
10. Quoting examples from this passage, explain the terms (a) antithesis, (b) asyndeton, (c) hendiadys, (d) anaphora, (e) tricolon.   <u>10</u>
    40

Caesar is besieging Avaricum. Though he has great problems obtaining supplies from friendly Gallic tribes, his soldiers refuse to use this as grounds for abandoning the siege.

de re frumentaria Boios atque Aeduos adhortari non destitit; quorum alteri, quod nullo   1
studio agebant, non multum adiuvabant, alteri non magnis facultatibus, quod civitas erat
exigua et infirma, celeriter quod habuerunt consumpserunt. summa difficultate rei
frumentariae adfecto exercitu tenuitate Boiorum, indiligentia Aeduorum, usque eo ut
complures dies frumento milites caruerint et pecore ex longinquioribus vicis adacto   5
extremam famem sustentarent, nulla tamen vox est ab eis audita populi Romani maiestate
et superioribus victoriis indigna. quin etiam Caesar cum in opere singulas legiones
appellaret et, si acerbius inopiam ferrent, se dimissurum oppugnationem diceret, universi
ab eo ne id faceret petebant: sic se complures annos illo imperante meruisse ut nullam
ignominiam acciperent, nusquam incepta re discederent: hoc se ignominiae laturos loco,   10
si inceptam oppugnationem reliquissent.

1. Why were the Boii and Aedui not giving Caesar much help with supply problems?   4
2. Who are *alteri* (1) and *alteri* (2)? Quote and translate the two words in the following sentence which show which is which.   3
3. *adfecto exercitu* (4): if this ablative absolute was translated by a clause with a finite verb, what English introductory word would be needed? Which Latin word later on shows this?   2
4. What were the results of the failure of the Gauls to supply food?   4
5. Suggest an appropriate translation for *vox* (6).   1
6. What offer does Caesar make to the soldiers in line 8?   2
7. Translate lines 8-9 *universi* to *petebant*.   2
8. What reasons do the soldiers give in lines 9-11 for refusing Caesar's offer?   5
9. Account for the mood and tense of *reliquissent* (11).   2
10. What are the meanings or uses of the ablative in *difficultate* (3), *tenuitate* (4), *frumento* (5), *maiestate* (6), *imperante* (9)?   5
                                                                                          30

*Alexander, king of Macedonia, and Darius III, king of Persia, manoeuvre before the
Battle of Issus in 333 BC.*

Isson deinde Alexander copias admovit, ubi consilio habito utrum ultra progrediendum   1
foret, an ibi exspectandi essent novi milites quos ex Macedonia advenire **constabat.**
Parmenion non alium locum proelio aptiorem esse censebat. quippe illic utriusque regis
copias numero futuras pares, cum angustiae multitudinem non caperent; planitiem ipsis
camposque esse vitandos, ubi circumiri possent. itaque rex inter angustias montium   5
hostem exspectare statuit.

      forte eadem nocte et Alexander ad **fauces** quibus Syria aditur, et Dareus ad eum
locum quem Amanicas Pylas vocant, pervenit. nec dubitavere Persae quin **Isso** relicta
Macedones fugerent; nam etiam **saucii** quidam et invalidi, qui agmen non poterant
persequi, excepti erant. quos omnes Dareus praecisis manibus circumduci, ut copias suas   10
noscerent, satisque omnibus spectatis, nuntiare quae vidissent regi suo iussit. motis ergo
castris, superat **Pinarum** amnem, in tergis, ut credebat, fugientium haesurus. at illi
quorum amputaverat manus ad exercitum Macedonum properant, Dareum, quanto
maximo cursu posset, sequi nuntiantes. itaque Alexander eo ipso loco **metari** suos castra
iussit, laetus in illis potissimum angustiis decernendum fore.   15

Line	1 & 8	Issus –i (acc. Isson) (fem.)	Issus, a city in southern Turkey at the foot of Mount Amanus on the Mediterranean
	2	constat (impersonal)	it is certain
	3	Parmenion –onis	Parmenion, one of Alexander's generals
	7	fauces –ium	pass, narrows
	9	saucius –a –um	wounded
	12	Pinarus –i	Pinarus, on whose banks the battle was fought
	14	metari	to lay out, pitch

1.   What decision does Alexander ponder in lines 1-2?   4
2.   Account for the difference in construction and meaning between *progrediendum*
     (1) and *exspectandi* (2).   4
3.   What was Parmenion's advice, and what was his reasoning?   2,5
4.   Why is *constabat* (2) indicative, but *possent* (5) subjunctive?   2
5.   Why did the Persians believe the Macedonians to be in flight?   3
6.   How did Darius treat his prisoners?   1
7.   Why did Darius have the prisoners led around his camp?   3
8.   Why did Darius cross the River Pinarus (12), and what is the point of *ut
     credebat*?   2,2
9.   Quote and translate the Latin word which shows Alexander's reaction to the
     message brought in lines 13-14. Why does he feel this way?   1,3
10.   What parts of the verb are *foret* (2), *dubitavere* (8), *haesurus* (12)?   3
                                                      35

Cicero, *De Officiis* III. xxii. 86-87

'If the things which seem most advantageous (utilia) are not so, because they are full of shame (dedecus) and are morally wrong, we should be quite convinced that nothing is advantageous which is not honourable.'

id quidem cum saepe **alias**, tum Pyrrhi bello a C. Fabricio consule iterum et a senatu   1
nostro iudicatum est. cum enim rex Pyrrhus populo Romano bellum ultro intulisset,
cumque de imperio certamen esset cum rege generoso ac potenti, perfuga ab eo venit in
castra Fabrici eique est pollicitus, si praemium sibi proposuisset, se, ut clam venisset, sic
clam in Pyrrhi castra rediturum et eum veneno necaturum. hunc Fabricius reducendum   5
curavit ad Pyrrhum, idque eius factum laudatum a senatu est. atqui, si speciem utilitatis
opinionemque quaerimus, magnum illud bellum perfuga unus et gravem adversarium
imperii sustulisset, sed magnum dedecus et flagitium, quocum laudis certamen fuisset,
eum non virtute sed scelere superatum.

utrum igitur utilius vel Fabricio, qui talis in hac urbe, qualis **Aristides** Athenis,   10
fuit, vel senatui nostro, qui numquam utilitatem a dignitate **seiunxit**, armis cum hoste
certare an venenis?

Line	1	alias	(adverb) at other times
	7	opinio –onis	what most people think
	10	Aristides	nicknamed 'the Just' for his absolute integrity
	11	seiungere	to separate

1. Line 1: for what does the abbreviation C. stand? What other information does the first sentence give us about Fabricius?   2
2. What does Cicero say was the motive for the war?   1
3. What promise does the deserter make to Fabricius? What does *ut* mean here (4) (Be careful!)?   4,1
4. What was Fabricius' reaction, and how did the Senate view it?   2
5. What is the effect of Cicero's word order and positioning in lines 7-8 (*magnum illud* to *flagitium*)?   3
6. Line 8 *sustulisset*: for what verb does *sustuli* in the meaning needed here supply the perfect forms, and what does the verb mean?   2
7. Lines 8-9: what would have been a shameful disgrace?   3
8. Precisely what part of *utilis* is *utilius* (10)?   2
9. In what case is *Athenis* (10)?   1
10. What are the meanings of *quidem* (1), *cum ... tum ...* (1), *ultro* (2), *atqui* (6), *vel ... vel ...* (10-11), *talis ... qualis ...* (10)?   6
11. *proposuisset* (4) and *fuisset* (8) are subjunctive for the same reason; what is it? Explain their reasons for being pluperfect.   1,2
    30

Caesar, *De Bello Gallico* IV. 1-2.

Part of Caesar's description of the Suebi, 'by far the largest and the most warlike tribe of all the Germans.'

hi centum **pagos** habere dicuntur, ex quibus quotannis singula milia armatorum bellandi 1
causa ex finibus educunt. reliqui qui domi manserunt se atque illos **alunt**; hi rursus in
vicem anno post in armis sunt, illi domi remanent. sic neque agri cultura nec ratio atque
usus belli intermittitur. mercatoribus est **aditus** magis eo ut quae bello ceperint quibus
vendant habeant, quam quod ullam rem ad se importari **desiderent**. quin etiam **iumentis**, 5
quibus maxime Galli delectantur quaeque maximo parant pretio, Germani importatis his
non utuntur sed quae sunt apud eos nata, haec cotidiana exercitatione ut sint summo
labori **idonea** efficiunt. equestribus proeliis saepe ex equis desiliunt ac pedibus pugnant,
nec turpius quicquam habetur quam **ephippiis** uti. itaque ad quemvis numerum
ephippiatorum equitum quamvis pauci adire audent. vinum ad se omnino importari non 10
sinunt, quod ea re ad laborem ferendum **remollescere** homines arbitrantur.

Line	1	pagus	canton, province
	2	alere + acc.	to grow food for
	4	aditus –us	access, permission to approach
	5	desiderare	to want
		iumentum –i	horse
	8	idoneus –a –um	fit for, capable of
	9	ephippium –i	saddle
	11	remollescere	to grow soft

1. How many men do the Suebi take to war each year?   1
2. Lines 1-4: explain how the Suebi kept agriculture going as well as the training and practice in war. What is the meaning of *in vicem*?   3
3. Why do they allow traders to come to them?   2
4. Lines 4-5: why are *ceperint*, *vendant* and *habeant* subjunctive?   3
5. Contrast the attitudes of the Gauls and Germans to horses (6-8).   5
6. What do the Suebi often do in cavalry battles?   2
7. Translate *nec turpius quicquam habetur* (9).   3
8. How do the Suebi show their scorn for riders who use saddles?   3
9. Why is the importing of wine totally banned?   2
10. Account for the cases of the following words: *domi* (2), *anno* (3), *mercatoribus* (4), *pretio* (6).   4
11. Compare the meanings of *bellandi* (1) and *ferendum* (11) in relation to their constructions.   2

30

Livy, V. 39.

390 BC The Gauls have overwhelmed a Roman army on the bank of the River Allia; now they are at the gates of Rome, and the Romans prepare for the expected attack.

cum defendi urbem posse tam parva relicta manu spes nulla esset, placuit cum 1
coniugibus ac liberis iuventutem militarem senatusque robur in arcem Capitoliumque
concedere, armisque et frumento conlato, ex loco inde munito deos hominesque et
Romanum nomen defendere; **flaminem sacerdotes**que Vestales sacra publica a caede, ab
incendiis procul auferre nec ante deseri cultum eorum quam non superessent qui colerent. 5
si arx Capitoliumque, sedes deorum, si senatus, caput publici consilii, si militaris
iuventus superfuerit imminenti ruinae urbis, facilem **iacturam** esse seniorum relictae in
urbe **utique** periturae turbae. et quo id aequiore animo de plebe multitudo ferret, senes
triumphales consularesque simul se cum illis palam dicere obituros, nec his corporibus,
quibus non arma ferre, non tueri patriam possent, oneraturos **inopiam** armatorum. 10

Line 4	flamen –inis	priest
	sacerdotes	i.e. the Vestal Virgins
7	iactura –ae	loss
8	utique	in any case
10	inopia	i.e. of food

1. Who were to take refuge on the Capitol? Why was this decision taken? 3,3
2. (a) What were the priest and Vestals to do? 5
    (b) Explain the use of *quam* here (5). 1
    (c) Account for the subjunctives *superessent* and *colerent* (5) (one explanation
    will not cover both). 2
3. In lines 6-8
    (a) What were the reasons for the importance of the survival of the Capitol,
    the Senate and the younger men? 3
    (b) Why were they not so concerned with the loss of the older men? 2
    (c) What part of what verb is *superfuerit* (7)? 1
4. (a) Why did the *senes* say publicly that they would die with them, and what
    reason did they give? 2,4
    (b) What is the point of *triumphales consularesque*? 2
    (c) Explain the use of the infinitive *dicere* (9). 2
    ___
    30

47

The story of Aratus of Sicyon.
Part 1: *A financial crisis that does not seem to have a just solution.*

at vero Aratus Sicyonius iure laudatur, qui, cum eius civitas quinquaginta annos a tyrannis 1
teneretur, profectus **Argis** Sicyonem clandestino introitu urbe est potitus, cumque
tyrannum Nicoclem improviso oppressisset, sescentos exsules, qui **locupletissimi** fuerant
eius civitatis, restituit remque publicam adventu suo liberavit. sed cum magnam
animadverteret in bonis et **possessionibus** difficultatem, quod et eos, quos ipse restituerat, 5
quorum bona alii possederant, **egere** iniquissimum esse arbitrabatur et quinquaginta
annorum **possessiones** moveri non nimis aequum putabat, propterea quod tam longo
spatio multa hereditatibus, multa emptionibus, multa **dotibus** tenebantur sine iniuria,
iudicavit neque illis adimi nec iis non **satis fieri**, quorum illa fuerant, oportere. 9

Line	2	Argi –orum	the city of Argos
	3	locuples –tis	wealthy
	5 & 7	possessio –nis	tenure, occupation
	6	egere	to be poor
	8	dos dotis	dowry
	9	satis facere	to make amends, reparation

1. Explain by what steps Aratus got control of the city of Sicyon (lines 2-3). 3
2. What was his first act when he had control (lines 3-4)? 2
3. Lines 4-7 (*putabat*): Explain the problem which faced Aratus. 5
4. Line 6: Account for the uses of the infinitives *egere* and *esse*. 2
5. Lines 7-8: What is Cicero referring to in *tam longo spatio*? 2
6. By what methods had much of the property changed hands? What does *sine iniuria* mean in this context? 2,1
7. Line 9: what decision did Aratus come to? Show clearly to whom or what *illis*, *iis* and *illa* refer. 4
8. Account for the cases of *Argis* (2), *urbe* (2), *spatio* (8), *illis* (9). 4
_____
25

Part 2: *How Aratus solved the crisis.*

cum igitur statuisset opus esse ad eam rem constituendam pecunia, Alexandream se   1
proficisci velle dixit remque integram ad reditum suum iussit esse, isque celeriter ad
Ptolemaeum, suum hospitem, venit, qui tum regnabat alter post Alexandream conditam.
cui cum exposuisset patriam se liberare velle causamque docuisset, a rege facile
impetravit ut grandi pecunia adiuvaretur. quam cum Sicyonem attulisset, adhibuit sibi in   5
consilium quindecim principes, cum quibus causas **cognovit** et eorum, qui aliena
tenebant, et eorum, qui sua amiserant, perfecitque aestimandis possessionibus, ut
persuaderet aliis, ut pecuniam accipere mallent, possessionibus **cederent**, aliis, ut
commodius putarent **numerari** sibi quam suum recuperare. ita perfectum est ut omnes
concordia constituta sine querella discederent.   10

Line 5	impetrare	to get (by asking)
6	cognoscere	to investigate
8	cedere + dat.	to give up a claim to
9	numerare	to pay in cash

1. Why did Aratus go to Alexandria?   1
2. What is the meaning of the phrase *opus est* (1)?   1
3. What information are we given about Ptolemy in line 3?   3
4. What did Aratus tell Ptolemy?   2
5. What was Ptolemy's reaction to this?   2
6. What does *principes* (6) mean in this context?   1
7. Two groups of people are mentioned in lines 6-7. Who are they?   2
8. What arrangements do these two groups accept in lines 8-9?   4
9. What was the result of Aratus's arrangements?   2
10. Compare the constructions and meanings of *ad* in lines 1-2 (*ad reditum*).   2
11. Compare the constructions and meanings of *quam* in lines 5 and 9.   2
12. Compare the constructions and meanings of *ut* in lines 7-8.   2
13. It has been said that Cicero often progresses in each section from a more
    narrative style to a higher rhetorical level. With close reference to the text,
    discuss this proposition with regard to both this passage and the preceding one.   6
                                                                                           ───
                                                                                            30

Caesar, *De Bello Gallico* III. 19.

The Gauls attack the camp of Titurius Sabinus, one of Caesar's commanders. They are carrying heavy loads of brushwood to put in the ditch, so that they can cross it.

locus erat castrorum editus et paulatim ab imo **acclivis** circiter passus mille. huc magno 1
cursu contenderunt, ut quam minimum spati ad se colligendos armandosque Romanis
daretur, exanimatique pervenerunt. Sabinus suos hortatus cupientibus signum dat.
impeditis hostibus propter ea quae ferebant onera, subito duabus portis eruptionem fieri
iubet. factum est opportunitate loci, hostium inscientia ac defatigatione, virtute militum et 5
superiorum pugnarum exercitatione, ut ne unum quidem nostrorum impetum ferrent ac
statim terga verterent. quos impeditos integris viribus milites nostri consecuti magnum
numerum eorum occiderunt; reliquos equites consectati paucos, qui ex fuga evaserant,
reliquerunt. sic uno tempore et de navali pugna Sabinus et de Sabini victoria Caesar
certior factus est; civitatesque omnes se statim Sabino dediderunt. nam ut ad bella 10
suscipienda Gallorum alacer ac promptus est animus, sic mollis ac minime resistens ad
calamitates perferendas mens eorum est.

Line 1	acclivis –e	sloping upwards

1.	What information are we given about the position of the camp?	3
2.	Why did the Gauls charge to the camp, and what effect did the charge have on them?	3,1
3.	Quote and translate the Latin word which shows the mood of the Romans.	1
4.	What factors affected the outcome of the fight, and what was the outcome of the first clash (4-7 *verterent*)?	4,2
5.	In line 7 what reasons does Caesar give for the Romans' superiority?	2
6.	What case is *equites* (8), and what part do they play in the battle?	3
7.	What comments does Caesar make about the character of the Gauls?	4
8.	What are the uses or meanings of *ut* and *ne* in lines 6 and 10?	3
9.	What cases are the following words, and why are they in these cases: *passus* (1), *spati* (2), *cupientibus* (3), *quae* (4)?	4
		30

Livy, IX. 2.

How the Samnites trapped a Roman army in the Caudine Forks. These consisted of a plain surrounded by mountains, with, at each end, a wooded pass. 'Into this plain by one pass the Romans marched their column down through a cleft in the cliffs ....'

in eum campum via alia per cavam rupem Romani demisso agmine cum ad alias   1
angustias protinus pergerent, **saeptas** deiectu arborum saxorumque ingentium obiacente
mole invenere. cum fraus hostilis apparuisset, praesidium etiam in summo saltu
conspicitur. citati inde retro, qua venerant, pergunt repetere viam; eam quoque clausam
sua obice armisque inveniunt. sistunt inde gradum sine ullius imperio, stuporque omnium   5
animos ac velut torpor quidam membra insolitus tenet, intuentesque alii alios, cum
alterum quisque **compotem** magis mentis ac consilii ducerent, diu immobiles silent;
deinde, quamquam ludibrio fore munientes perditis rebus ac spe omni adempta
cernebant, tamen, ne culpam malis adderent, pro se quisque, nec hortante ullo nec
imperante, ad muniendum versi castra prope aquam vallo circumdant. ad consules   10
maestos, ne advocantes quidem in consilium, quando nec consilio nec auxilio locus esset,
sua sponte legati ac tribuni conveniunt, militesque ad praetorium versi opem, quam vix di
immortales ferre poterant, ab ducibus exposcunt.

Line	2	saepire	to enclose, block
	7	compos + gen.	in control of

1. What did the Romans see as they approached the other pass?   3
2. (a) What is the meaning of *ob-* on *obiacente* (2)?   1
    (b) What part of the verb is *invenere* (3)?   1
3. How did the Romans react when they
    (a) realised the enemy's trap (3-4)?   2
    (b) found the first pass blocked (4-6 *tenet*)?   3
4. Translate *intuentes alii alios* (6).   2
5. Show how in lines 5-7 (*sistunt ... silent*) Livy uses sound, choice of word, and
    word order to add dramatic weight and to emphasise the most important words.   5
6. Express lines 6-7 (*cum ... ducerent*) in your own words. How can *quisque* be
    nominative with a plural verb?   3,1
7. Account for the case of *ludibrio* (8).   1
8. Show with close reference to the text how in lines 8-13 Livy repeatedly
    emphasises the hopelessness of the Romans' position.   6
9. What was the *praetorium* (12)?   1
10. Compare the uses of *suus* in lines 5 and 12.   2
11. What do the following words or phrases mean: *protinus* (2), *retro* (4), *ne ...*
    quidem (11), *sua sponte* (12)?   4
                                                                                        ⎯⎯
                                                                                        35

After the battle of Issus Alexander captured the family of Darius, king of Persia, and treated them with kindness and consideration. Now (332 BC) Darius has sent envoys to negotiate a peace treaty and the return of his family.

Alexander legatis excedere tabernaculo iussis, quid placeret, ad consilium refert. diu 1
nemo quid sentiret ausus est dicere, incerta regis voluntate; tandem **Parmenio** ait se
magnopere censere, ut unam **anum** et duas puellas, itinerum agminumque impedimenta,
xxx milibus **talentum** auri **permutet**. ingrata oratio regi fuit; itaque, ut finem dicendi fecit:
'et ego', inquit, 'pecuniam quam gloriam mallem, si Parmenio essem; nunc Alexander de 5
paupertate securus sum et me non mercatorem memini esse, sed regem. nihil quidem
habeo **venale**, sed fortunam meam **utique** non vendo. captivos si placet reddi, honestius
dono dabimus quam pretio remittemus'.

    introductis deinde legatis, ad hunc modum respondit: 'nuntiate Dareo me, quae
fecerim clementer et liberaliter, non amicitiae eius **tribuisse**, sed naturae meae. bellum 10
cum captivis et feminis gerere non soleo; armatus sit oportet quem oderim. quodsi saltem
pacem bona fide peteret, deliberarem forsitan an darem. verum enimvero, cum modo
milites meos litteris ad proditionem, modo amicos ad perniciem meam pecunia sollicitet, ad
internecionem mihi persequendus est, non ut iustus hostis sed ut **percussor veneficus**'.

Line	2	Parmenio –onis	Parmenio, a general of Alexander
	3	anus –us	old woman
	4	talentum –i (gen. plur. –um)	talent, probably a weight of roughly 60 pounds or 27 kilos
		permutare	to exchange
	7	venalis –e	for sale
		utique	in any case
	10	tribuere	to ascribe, attribute
	14	internecio –onis	extermination
		percussor veneficus	assassin who uses poison

1.   What question did Alexander put to his council, and why did nobody dare to reply for some time?   2

2.   Apart from the ransom money, why would Parmenio like to be rid of Darius' family?   2

3.   Lines 5-8: On what grounds does Alexander reject the ransom?   4

4.   In lines 9-14 what is Alexander's attitude towards Darius?   4

5.   Why does Alexander not believe Darius' offer of peace to be genuine?   3

6.   What impression do you get of Alexander from this piece? You must support your judgements with evidence from the text.   5

7.   Account for the cases of *talentum* (4), *dono* (8), *pretio* (8), *mihi* (14).   4

8.   Compare the meanings of *ut* in lines 4 and 14.   2

9.   What are the meanings of *quodsi* (11), *saltem* (11), *verum* (12), *modo ... modo ...* (12-13)?   <u>4</u>

                                                    30

Sallust, *Catiline* 61.

5 January 62 BC Catiline and his rebel army have been wiped out by government forces.

sed confecto proelio tum vero cerneres, quanta audacia quantaque animi vis fuisset in 1
exercitu Catilinae. nam fere quem quisque vivus pugnando locum ceperat, eum amissa
anima corpore tegebat. pauci autem, quos medios cohors praetoria disiecerat, paulo
diversius sed omnes tamen adversis vulneribus conciderant. Catilina vero longe a suis
inter hostium cadavera repertus est, paululum etiam spirans ferociamque animi, quam 5
habuerat vivus, in vultu retinens. postremo ex omni copia neque in proelio neque in fuga
quisquam civis **ingenuus** captus est: ita cuncti suae hostiumque vitae **iuxta** pepercerant.
neque tamen exercitus populi Romani laetam aut incruentam victoriam adeptus erat. nam
strenuissimus quisque aut occiderat in proelio aut graviter vulneratus discesserat. multi
autem, qui e castris visendi aut spoliandi gratia processerant, volventes hostilia cadavera 10
amicum alii pars hospitem aut cognatum reperiebant; fuere item qui inimicos suos
cognoscerent. ita varie per omnem exercitum laetitia maeror, luctus atque gaudia
agitabantur.

Line 7	ingenuus	free born
	iuxta	equally little

1. In lines 2-3
   (a) how does Sallust show the courage of Catiline's army? 3
   (b) account for the case of *pugnando*. 1
2. What had happened to a few of the men, and how was their courage shown? 3
3. How does Sallust show Catiline's determination in lines 4-6? 4
4. Explain in your own words what Sallust means by *cuncti suae hostiumque vitae iuxta pepercerant* (7). 2
5. What casualties had the state's forces suffered? 2
6. Why did many leave the camp? 2
7. *ita varie per omnem exercitum laetitia maeror* (12): why did the army have mixed feelings, and what is the difference between *hostes* (7) and *inimici* (11)? 4,1
8. Account for the subjunctives *cerneres* (1) and *cognoscerent* (12). 2
9. Where in lines 8-13 does Sallust employ (a) litotes, (b) variation in expression, (c) chiasmus? 3
   What, in each case, is the effect of these techniques? 3
   30

Pliny, II. 20.

Three stories about Regulus, a legacy hunter (captator). *Such men courted* (captare)
the old and sick, trying to be included in their wills.
Part 1: *How Regulus tricked Verania.*

Verania, Pisonis uxor, graviter iacebat, ad hanc Regulus venit. primum impudentiam   1
hominis, qui venerit ad aegram, cuius marito **inimicissimus**, ipsi invisissimus fuerat! **esto**,
si venit tantum; at ille etiam proximus **toro** sedit, quo die qua hora nata esset interrogavit.
ubi audiit, componit vultum intendit oculos movet **labra**, agitat digitos computat. nihil. ut
diu miseram exspectatione suspendit, 'habes' inquit '**climactericum** tempus sed evades.   5
quod ut tibi magis **liqueat**, **haruspicem** consulam, quem sum frequenter expertus.' nec
mora, sacrificium facit, adfirmat **exta** cum siderum significatione **congruere**. illa, ut in
periculo **credula**, poscit codicillos, **legatum** Regulo scribit. mox ingravescit, clamat
moriens hominem **nequam** perfidum ac plus etiam quam **periurum** qui sibi per salutem
filii periurasset.   10

Line 2	inimicissimus	according to Tacitus, after Piso was murdered, Regulus bit Piso's head and rewarded his murderer.
	esto	'so be it', meaning 'That would be bad enough ...'
3	torus –i	couch
4	labrum –i	lip
5	climactericum	according to astrologers, the 'critical times' in a person's life were the multiples of seven years.
6	liquet	it is clear, sure
	haruspex –icis	soothsayer
7	exta –orum	internal organs, entrails
	congruere	to agree
8	credulus –a –um	ready to believe
	legatum –i	legacy
9	nequam (indeclinable)	worthless
	periurus –a –um	perjured, having broken an oath or promise.

1. What are we told about Verania in the first sentence?   2
2. (a) Why is *impudentiam* (1) accusative?   1
    (b) Why is *venerit* (2) subjunctive?   1
    (c) What does Pliny regard as shameless behaviour?   3
3. What does *tantum* mean in line 3?   1
4. What did Regulus do when he arrived?   3
5. Lines 4-5: Explain how Regulus builds up the suspense and engages Verania's
    interest, and how Pliny does the same to us.   4,2
6. Line 6: In what way does this purpose/final clause breach the usual rules?   1
7. Explain the grammar of *nec mora* (6-7). How should it be translated into
    idiomatic English?   2
8. What did Regulus learn by making a sacrifice?   2
9. Quote the Latin and translate the promise Regulus had made which causes
    Verania to call him *periurus* (9).   2

10. (a) To whom does *sibi* (9) refer?   1
    (b) How had Regulus reinforced his oath?   1
    (c) On what two grounds is *periurasset* subjunctive?   2
11. Compare the meanings of *ut* in lines 4 and 7.   2
                                        30

P.S. *delicta maiorum immeritus lues* – Horace, *Odes* III. vi. 1.
Regulus' son died when still young. Regulus himself rose from poverty and obscurity to become immensely rich.

Pliny, II. 20

Part 2*: Regulus gets what he deserves.*

Velleius Blaesus ille **locuples** consularis novissima valetudine conflictabatur; cupiebat   1
mutare **testamentum**. Regulus qui speraret aliquid ex novis tabulis, quia nuper captare
eum coeperat, medicos hortari rogare, quoquo modo spiritum homini **prorogarent**.
postquam signatum est **testamentum**, mutat personam, vertit adlocutionem, isdemque
medicis '**quousque** miserum cruciatis? quid **invidetis** bona morte, cui dare vitam non   5
potestis?' moritur Blaesus et, tamquam omnia audisset, Regulo ne tantulum quidem.
   Aurelia ornata femina signatura **testamentum** sumpserat pulcherrimas tunicas.
Regulus cum venisset ad signandum, 'rogo' inquit 'has mihi **leges**.' Aurelia ludere
hominem putabat, ille serio instabat; ne multa, coegit mulierem aperire tabulas ac sibi
tunicas quas erat induta **legare**; observavit scribentem, inspexit an scripsisset. et Aurelia   10
quidem vivit, ille tamen istud tamquam morituram coegit.

Line	1	locuples –tis	wealthy
	2 etc	testamentum –i	will
	3	prorogare	to prolong
	5	quousque	for how long
		invidere + abl.	to prevent, deny
	8 & 10	legare	to bequeath, leave

1. What is the meaning of *ille* here?   1
2. What are we told about Blaesus' state of health?   2
3. Why did Regulus hope for something from the new will? Why is *speraret*
    subjunctive?   2,1
4. Explain the use of the infinitives *hortari rogare*.   2
5. Line 4 *mutat personam*: explain how Regulus changed character.   4
6. Why did Regulus go to see Aurelia?   1
7. Why is *leges* (8) subjunctive?   1
8. What was Aurelia's reaction to Regulus' request?   1
9. Explain the syntax of *ne multa* (9) and give an idiomatic translation of it.   2
10. Lines 9-10: how did Regulus make sure that Aurelia included him in her will?   3
11. Why, as Pliny writes, has Regulus received nothing from Blaesus or Aurelia?   2
12. Translate *tamquam omnia audisset* (6) and *tamquam morituram* (11).   <u>3</u>
                                                                                            25

Livy, XXXVII. 4. 8.

The Roman general, Acilius, is based in the Greek city of Elatia. In a surprise move he launches an attack on Lamia and, after unexpectedly determined resistance, eventually captures it.

Acilius autem Lamiam aggredi constituit, ratus oppidanos, quod nihil tale timerent, 1
incautos opprimi posse. profectus igitur ab Elatia primum in hostium terra circum
Sphercheum amnem posuit castra; inde nocte motis signis prima luce corona moenia
oppugnavit.

      magnus pavor ac tumultus, ut in re improvisa, fuit. constantius tamen, quam quis 5
eos facturos esse crederet, in tam subito periculo, cum viri propugnarent, feminae tela
omnis generis saxaque in muros gererent, urbem eo die defenderunt. Acilius, signo
receptui dato, suos in castra medio die reduxit; et tum cibo et quiete refectis corporibus,
nuntiavit ut ante lucem armati paratique essent; nisi urbem expugnavissent, se eos in castra
non reducturum. eodem tempore, quo pridie, pluribus locis aggressus, cum oppidanos 10
iam vires, iam tela, iam ante omnia animus deficeret, intra paucas horas urbem cepit.

1.   On what grounds did Acilius think his attack on Lamia would be successful?   2
2.   What is unusual about the grammar of *ab Elatia* (2)?   1
3.   What information does Livy give us about where Acilius pitched camp?   2
4.   Explain what is meant by the phrase *motis signis* (3).   2
5.   Translate *in re improvisa* (5) into idiomatic English.   2
6.   Lines 5-7: what does Livy tell us about the reactions of the citizens and how they
     defended the town? What is the use or meaning of the subjunctive *crederet*?   6,1
7.   Account for the cases of *signo* (7) and *receptui* (8).   2
8.   In line 9 what construction is introduced by *ut*? Explain the point of the tense
     of *parati essent*.   2
9.   What threat does Acilius issue in lines 9-10?   3
10.   Translate *eodem tempore, quo pridie* (10).   2
11.   Why was the attack the next day successful?   4
12.   Explain the force of the prepositions on *oppugnavit* (4) and *expugnavissent* (9).   2
13.   Account for the mood and tense of *timerent* (1) and *expugnavissent* (9).   <u>4</u>
                                                                  35

Cicero, *In Catilinam* III. 2. 5-6.

3 December 63 BC *Catiline has fled from Rome, and his associates who stayed in Rome have invited some envoys of the Gallic Allobroges to participate in the plot to overthrow the government in Rome.*
Part 1: *Cicero describes to the people how he laid an ambush for the Allobroges, to seize compromising letters to Catiline signed by the chief plotters.*

itaque hesterno die L. Flaccum et C. Pomptinum praetores ad me vocavi, rem exposui, 1
quid fieri placeret ostendi. illi autem, qui omnia de republica praeclara et egregia
sentirent, sine recusatione ac sine ulla mora negotium susceperunt et, cum
advesperasceret, occulte ad pontem Mulvium pervenerunt atque ibi in proximis villis ita
bipertito fuerunt, ut Tiberis inter eos et pons interesset. eodem autem et ipsi sine 5
cuiusquam suspicione multos fortes viros eduxerant, et ego complures delectos
adulescentes, quorum opera utor assidue in re publica, praesidio cum gladiis miseram.
  interim tertia fere vigilia exacta, cum iam pontem magno comitatu legati
Allobrogum ingredi inciperent unaque Volturcius, fit in eos impetus; educuntur et ab illis
gladii et a nostris. res praetoribus erat nota solis, ignorabatur a ceteris. tum interventu 10
Pomptini atque Flacci pugna, quae erat commissa, sedatur. litterae, quaecumque erant in
eo comitatu, integris signis praetoribus traduntur: ipsi comprehensi ad me, cum iam
dilucesceret, deducuntur.

1.   When did Cicero summon Flaccus and Pomptinus?   1
2.   Translate quid *fieri placeret ostendi* (2) into natural English.   2
3.   What compliment does Cicero pay Flaccus and Pomptinus in lines 2-3?   3
4.   Describe, as precisely as possible, where Flaccus and Pomptinus took up their positions.   4
5.   Account for the cases of *opera* and *praesidio* (7).   2
6.   (a) When in modern terms did the envoys of the Allobroges cross the bridge?   1
     (b) Whom did they have with them?   2
     (c) What is the meaning of *una* (9)?   1
7.   Give an appropriate translation of *res* in line 10.   1
8.   In line 11 why has Cicero written *quaecumque* rather than simply *quae*, and what is the point of *integris signis* (12)?   1,2
9.   Account for the subjunctives *sentirent* (3) and *interesset* (5).   2
10.   What is the meaning of *-sco* as a verbal ending? What do *advesperascit* (4) and *dilucescit* (13) mean? (cf. *adulescentes*)   <u>3</u>
                                                        25

Cicero, *In Catilinam* III. 3. 7-8.

Part 2: *Cicero describes the discussion about what to do with the letters, the seizure of arms from the house of Cethegus, one of the plotters, and the questioning before the Senate of Volturcius, who was apprehended with the envoys of the Allobroges.*

cum summis et clarissimis huius civitatis viris, qui audita re **frequentes** ad me mane 1
convenerant, litteras a me prius aperiri quam ad senatum **deferri** placeret, ne, si nihil
esset inventum, **temere** a me tantus tumultus iniectus civitati videretur, negavi me esse
facturum, ut de periculo publico non ad consilium publicum rem integram **deferrem**.
etenim, **Quirites**, si ea, quae erant ad me **delata**, reperta non essent, tamen ego non 5
arbitrabar in tantis rei publicae periculis esse mihi nimiam diligentiam pertimescendam.
senatum **frequentem** celeriter, ut vidistis, coegi. atque interea statim admonitu
Allobrogum C. Sulpicium praetorem, fortem virum, misi, qui ex aedibus Cethegi, si quid
telorum esset, efferret.
introduxi Volturcium sine Gallis, hortatus sum ut ea quae sciret sine timore 10
indicaret. tum ille dixit se habere ad Catilinam mandata et litteras, ut servorum praesidio
uteretur, ut ad urbem quam primum cum exercitu accederet; id autem eo consilio, ut, cum
urbem ex omnibus partibus incendissent caedemque infinitam civium fecissent, **praesto**
esset ille, qui et fugientes exciperet et se cum his urbanis ducibus coniungeret.

Line	1	frequens	in large numbers
	2 etc	deferre	to deliver, report
	3	temere	without good reason
	5	Quirites	Roman citizens
	7	frequens	in a full meeting
	13	praesto (adverb)	at hand

1. Lines 1-4:
    (a) Why do you think Cicero lays stress on the type of people who gathered at
    his house?   2
    (b) Account for the case of *viris* (1).   1
    (c) Explain the use of *quam* in line 2.   1
    (d) What was the view of these men?   3
    (e) Why did they take this view?   3
    (f) Account for the mood and tense of *esset inventum* (3)   2
2. What is Cicero's answer to their recommendation?   3
3. What reason does Cicero give for his decision in lines 5-6?   5
4. Line 9: account for (a) the case of *telorum*, (b) the mood of *efferret*.   2
5. What does *quam primum* (12) mean?   1
6. What parts in the attack on Rome are going to be played by (a) the conspirators
    in Rome, (b) Catiline?   2,2
7. Distinguish between the uses of *ut* in line 7 and twice in line 12.   <u>3</u>
                                                                                   30

Pliny, VIII. 24.

The Roman province of Achaea was largely the classical Hellas. As a mark of respect many of its cities had been allowed self government in internal affairs; but these affairs were now in disorder, and Valerius Maximus has been sent out as governor of Achaea with a special commission to sort out the problems.

sit apud te honor antiquitati, sit ingentibus factis, sit fabulis quoque. nihil ex cuiusquam dignitate, nihil ex libertate, nihil etiam ex **iactatione decerpseris**. habe ante oculos hanc esse terram, quae nobis miserit iura, quae leges non victis sed **petentibus** dederit, Athenas esse quas adeas, Lacedaemonem esse quam regas; quibus reliquam umbram et residuum libertatis nomen eripere durum ferum barbarum est. vides a medicis, quamquam in 5 adversa valetudine nihil servi ac liberi differant, mollius tamen liberos clementiusque tractari. **recordare** quid quaeque civitas fuerit, non ut despicias quod esse desierit; absit superbia asperitas. nec timueris contemptum. an contemnitur qui imperium qui fasces habet, nisi humilis et sordidus, et qui se primus ipse contemnit? male vim suam potestas aliorum **contumeliis** experitur, male terrore veneratio adquiritur, longeque valentior amor 10 ad obtinendum quod velis quam timor. nam timor abit si recedas, manet amor, ac sicut ille in odium hic in reverentiam vertitur.

Line	2	iactatio –onis	vanity, boasting
		decerpere	to take away
	3	petentibus	Livy records that in 450 BC the Romans sought advice from the Athenians about drafting the Twelve Tables of civil law.
	7	recordari	to remember
	10	contumelia –ae	insult

1. What is Maximus to respect in line 1?   3
2. What is Maximus always to bear in mind?   4
3. Lines 4-5:
   (a) explain what Pliny means by *reliquam umbram et residuum libertatis nomen*.   2
   (b) account for the cases of *quibus* and *durum*.   2
4. Explain the points of comparison in lines 5-7 to the positions and behaviour of Maximus and the Greek cities.   4
5. What part of the verb is *recordare* (7)?   1
6. Under what circumstances is the holder of supreme power liable to be despised?   2
7. In lines 9-12: (a) what advice does Pliny give Maximus about how to treat the provincials and what reasons does he give? (b) what are the meanings here of *sicut* and *ille … hic*?   4,2
8. Accounts for the subjunctives *sit* (1), *decerpseris* (2), *differant* (6).   3
9. Identify in the passage three features typical of a rhetorical style.   3

                                                                                          30

Caesar, *De Bello Civili* I. 40.

Fabius is Caesar's general in Spain; Petreius and Afranius are Pompey's. Fabius has built two bridges across the river, and Afranius one.

Fabius suis pontibus pabulatum mittebat, quod ea quae citra flumen fuerant superioribus 1
diebus consumpserat. hoc idem fere atque eadem de causa Pompeiani exercitus duces
faciebant, crebroque inter se equestribus proeliis contendebant. huc cum cotidiana
consuetudine egressae pabulatoribus praesidio propiore ponte legiones Fabianae duae
flumen transissent omnisque equitatus sequeretur, subito vi ventorum et aquae 5
magnitudine pons est interruptus et reliqua multitudo equitum interclusa. quo cognito a
Petreio et Afranio ex aggere atque **cratibus** quae flumine ferebantur, celeriter suo ponte
Afranius, legiones IIII equitatumque omnem traiecit duabusque Fabianis occurrit
legionibus. cuius adventu nuntiato L. Plancus, qui legionibus Fabianis praeerat,
necessaria re coactus locum capit superiorem diversamque aciem in duas partes constituit 10
ne ab equitatu circumveniri posset. ita congressus impari numero magnos impetus
legionum equitatusque sustinet. commisso ab equitibus proelio signa legionum duarum
procul ab utrisque conspiciuntur, quas C. Fabius ulteriore ponte subsidio nostris miserat,
suspicatus fore id quod accidit, ut duces adversariorum occasione et beneficio fortunae
ad nostros opprimendos uterentur. quarum adventu proelium dirimitur ac suas uterque 15
legiones reducit in castra.

Line 7	cratis –is	woodwork, timber

1. (a) For what was Fabius using the bridges, and why was this necessary?   3
   (b) Explain the syntax of *pabulatum*.   2
2. Quote and translate the words in lines 3 and 4 which tell you that the crossing
   of the river and skirmishing were regular occurrences (not verbs).   2
3. Why did two of Fabius' legions cross the river?   2
4. What broke down the bridge, and what was the effect on Fabius' forces?   2,2
5. How did Petreius and Afranius learn of the breaking of the bridge?   2
6. What were the tactics of Plancus against Afranius' forces, and what was his
   reason for these tactics?   3,2
7. Account for the cases of *subsidio* and *nostris* (13).   2
8. (a) What had Fabrius suspected?   3
   (b) Explain the syntax of *suspicatus fore id quod accidit ut*.   3
9. Explain why *utrisque* (13) is plural, and *uterque* (15) singular.   2
       30

Sallust, *Catiline 6.*

Sallust recounts the origins of Rome and its early successes.

urbem Romam, sicuti ego accepi, condidere atque habuere initio Troiani, qui Aenea duce 1
profugi sedibus incertis vagabantur, cumque eis **Aborigines**, genus hominum agreste,
sine legibus, sine imperio, liberum atque solutum. hi postquam in una moenia convenere,
dispari genere dissimili lingua, alii alio more viventes, incredibile memoratu est quam
facile **coaluerint**. sed postquam res eorum, civibus moribus agris aucta, satis prospera 5
satisque pollens videbatur, invidia ex **opulentia** orta est. igitur reges populique finitimi
bello temptare, pauci ex amicis auxilio esse; nam ceteri metu perculsi a periculis aberant.
at Romani domi militiaeque intenti festinare, parare, alius alium hortari, hostibus obviam
ire, libertatem patriam parentesque armis tegere. post ubi pericula virtute propulerant,
sociis atque amicis auxilia portabant, magisque dandis quam accipiendis beneficiis 10
amicitias parabant.

Line 2	Aborigines	original inhabitants of Latium
5	coalescere	to unite
6	opulentia –ae	wealth

1. What information are we given about (a) the Trojans, (b) the Aborigines?   3,3
2. (a) What factors were against the coalition of the Trojans and Aborigines?   3
   (b) What part of the verb is *convenere* (3)?   1
3. Translate *incredibile memoratu est*, and explain the syntax of *memoratu*.   2,2
4. What does Sallust see as the marks of Rome's power and prosperity, and what
   were the results of this prosperity (5-7)?   2,2
5. Why did only a few of Rome's friends give help?   1
6. (a) How did the Romans react to this threat from their neighbours?   4
   (b) Explain the use of the infinitives in lines 8-9.   1
7. What is unusual about the tense of *propulerant* (9)?   1
8. What change was there in Rome's foreign policy after the threat had been
   countered?   3
9. Account for the cases of *duce* (1), *auxilio* (7), *militiae* (8).   3
10. Translate the phrases *alii alio more viventes* (4) and *alius alium hortari* (8)
    into natural English.   4
                                                                                               ——
                                                                                               35

Cicero, *Ad Familiares* VIII. 14.

Caelius writes from Rome to Cicero. He anticipates the Civil War and shows himself a cynical political opportunist.

de summa re publica saepe tibi scripsi me ad annum pacem non videre, et quo propius ea contentio, quam fieri necesse est, accedit, eo clarius id periculum apparet. **propositum** hoc est, de quo qui rerum potiuntur sunt **dimicaturi**, quod Cn. Pompeius constituit non pati C. Caesarem consulem aliter fieri nisi exercitum et provincias tradiderit; Caesari autem persuasum est se salvum esse non posse si ab exercitu recesserit; fert illam tamen   5
condicionem, ut ambo exercitus tradant.

neque mearum rerum quid consilii capiam reperio; quod non dubito quin te quoque haec deliberatio sit perturbatura. nam mihi cum **hominibus his** et gratia et necessitudines sunt; causam **illam** amo unde homines odi. **illud te non** arbitror **fugere**, quin homines in dissensione domestica debeant, quamdiu civiliter sine armis certetur,   10
honestiorem sequi partem, ubi ad bellum et castra ventum sit, firmiorem, et id melius statuere quod tutius sit. in hac discordia video Cn. Pompeium senatum **quique res iudicant** secum habiturum, ad Caesarem omnes qui cum timore aut mala spe vivant accessuros; exercitum conferendum non esse. omnino satis spatii est ad considerandas utriusque copias et eligendam partem.   15

Line	2	propositum	main issue
	3	dimicare	to fight it out
	8	hominibus his	Caesar's supporters
	9	illam	Pompey's
		illud te non fugit	it does not escape your notice
	12-13	qui res iudicant	who supply the juries

1. How long does Caelius think that peace can last?   1
2. Translate *quam fieri necesse est* (2) into idiomatic English.   2
3. What does Caelius see as the main issues on the two sides, and what compromise has Caesar proposed?   5,1
4. Account for the subjunctive *capiam* (7).   2
5. Translate lines 7-8 *non dubito* to *perturbatura*.   3
6. What is Caelius's attitude to the two sides in lines 8-9?   4
7. What does Caelius see as the policy to be followed in cases of internal conflict?   6
8. Who are the supporters of each side, and on what criterion will Caelius decide who gets his support?   3,1
9. Compare the meanings of *res* in lines 1, 3 and 7.   3
10. Account for the cases of *eo* (2), *rerum* (7), *consilii* (7), *id* (11).   4
                                                                                            ――
                                                                                            35

Sallust, Catiline 36.

63 BC Catiline has left Rome to join Manlius and an army of ten thousand, and to lead them in an attempt to overthrow the state. Cicero and Antonius are the consuls.

haec ubi Romae comperta sunt, senatus Catilinam et Manlium hostes iudicat, ceterae 1
multitudini diem statuit, ante quam **sine fraude** liceret ab armis discedere. praeterea
decernit, uti consules dilectum habeant, Antonius cum exercitu Catilinam persequi
maturet, Cicero urbi praesidio sit.
     ea tempestate mihi imperium populi Romani multo maxime miserabile visum est. 5
cui cum ad occasum ab ortu solis **omnia domita** armis parerent, domi otium atque
divitiae, quae prima mortales putant, adfluerent, fuere tamen cives, qui seque remque
publicam obstinatis animis perditum irent. namque duobus senatus decretis ex tanta
multitudine neque praemio inductus coniurationem patefecerat neque ex castris Catilinae
quisquam omnium discesserat; tanta vis morbi plerosque civium animos invaserat. neque 10
solum illis **aliena** mens erat, qui conscii coniurationis fuerant, sed omnino cuncta plebs
novarum rerum studio Catilinae incepta probabat.

Line	2	sine fraude	without harm, under an amnesty
	6	omnia	everything = the whole world
		domare domitum	to tame
	11	alienus	diseased, insane

1. Lines 1-4:
   (a) what measures did the Senate pass to counter the threat of Catiline's army? 6
   (b) comment on the gender of *diem* (2). 1
2. Lines 5-8:
   (a) explain why Sallust describes the Roman empire as *miserabile*. 4
   (b) what does *cum* mean here? 1
   (c) what does Sallust mean by *ad occasum ab ortu solis*? 2
   (d) explain the syntax of *perditum*. 2
3. Lines 8-10:
   (a) what two facts show the strength of the disaffection felt by many of the citizens? 2
   (b) what two factors might have been expected to change the situation? 2
4. Lines 10-12:
   (a) how does Sallust emphasise the extent of the disaffection? 2
   (b) what does *novae res* mean in modern terms? 1
5. Account for the cases of *praesidio* (4), *multo* (5), *cui* (6), *domi* (6), *omnium* (10). 5
6. Account for the subjunctives *liceret* (2) and *irent* (8). 2
                                                                                          ——
                                                                                          30

Pliny, VI. xvi. 4-11.

Pliny is writing to the historian Tacitus, describing the heroism of his uncle during the eruption of Vesuvius in 79 AD.

erat Miseni classemque imperio praesens regebat. nonum kal. Septembres hora fere   1
septima mater mea indicat ei apparere nubem inusitata et magnitudine et specie. magnum
propiusque noscendum ut eruditissimo viro visum. iubet **liburnicam** aptari; mihi si venire
una vellem facit copiam; respondi studere me malle, et forte ipse quod scriberem dederat.

egrediebatur domo; accipit codicillos Rectinae imminenti periculo exterritae (nam   5
villa eius subiacebat, nec ulla nisi navibus fuga): ut se tanto discrimini eriperet orabat.
deducit quadriremes, ascendit ipse non Rectinae modo sed multis aliis laturus auxilium.
properat illuc unde alii fugiunt, rectumque cursum recta gubernacula in periculum tenet.
iam navibus cinis incidebat, quo propius accederent, calidior et densior; iam pumices
etiam nigrique et ambusti et fracti igne lapides; iam **vadum** subitum ruinaque montis   10
litora obstantia. cunctatus paulum an retro flecteret, mox gubernatori ut ita faceret
monenti 'fortes' inquit 'fortuna iuvat: **Pomponianum** pete.'

Line 3	liburnica	a small, fast sailing-boat
10	vadum –i	shallows
12	Pomponianus	another friend in the danger area

1. What was the job of Pliny's uncle?   1
2. When, in modern terms, did the eruption take place?   3
3. Explain the case and meaning of *noscendum* (3).   2
4. Explain the use of *ut* in line 3.   2
5. Translate lines 3-4 *mihi* to *copiam*. Account for the mood and tense of *vellem*.   3,2
6. Why was Rectina in extreme danger, and what did she ask Pliny's uncle to do?   2,2
7. Line 7 *laturus*: what part of what verb is this, and what is its meaning here?   2
8. Describe in detail what happened as the ships approached the danger area?   6
9. Explain the meaning of *ut ita faceret* (11) here.   2
10. Why are the following subjunctives: *scriberem* (4), *eriperet* (6), *flecteret* (11)?   ·   1,1,2
11. Account for the cases of the following words: *Miseni* (1), *magnitudine* (2), *Rectinae* (5), *discrimini* (6), *navibus* (9), *quo* (9).   6
12. Quote and identify three features of lines 9-12 which indicate that Pliny and his uncle had had rhetorical training.   <u>3</u>
                                                                                                 40

65

Tacitus, *Agricola* 38. 2-4.

Tacitus describes the scene after the devastating Roman victory over the Caledonians at Mons Graupius, and the subsequent actions of Agricola.

proximus dies faciem victoriae latius aperuit: vastum ubique silentium, secreti colles,   1
fumantia procul tecta, nemo exploratoribus obvius. quibus in omnem partem dimissis, ubi
incerta fugae vestigia neque usquam **conglobari** hostes compertum et exacta iam aestate
spargi bellum nequibat, in fines Borestorum exercitum deducit. ibi acceptis obsidibus,
praefecto classis circumvehi Britanniam praecipit. datae ad id vires, et praecesserat terror.   5
ipse peditem atque equites lento itinere, quo novarum gentium animi ipsa transitus mora
terrerentur, in hibernis locavit. et simul classis secunda tempestate ac fama Trucculensem
portum tenuit.

Line 3	conglobare	to collect
4	spargere	to spread

1. What indications were there of the totality of the victory?   4
2. Lines 1-2: comment on Tacitus's choice of vocabulary and use of language.   4
3. What does Tacitus mean by *incerta fugae vestigia* (3)?   2
4. Account for the ending of *compertum* (3). What does the verb mean?   2
5. Why could the war not be spread over a wider area?   1
6. What can you deduce from *deducit* (4) and line 5 about where the Boresti
   lived? Explain your answer.   2
7. What was the commander ordered to do, and what help did he have in this task?   1,2
8. What reason does Tacitus give for *lento itinere* (6)? Account for the
   subjunctive *terrerentur* (7).   3,1
9. Translate *secunda tempestate ac fama* (7).   <u>3</u>
                                                                                                   25

Sallust, *Catiline* 25.

*After listing men who were involved in Catiline's conspiracy to overthrow the state
(63 BC), Sallust adds that there were also women involved.*

Sed in eis erat Sempronia, quae multa saepe virilis audaciae facinora commiserat. haec 1
mulier genere atque forma, praeterea viro, liberis satis fortunata fuit; litteris Graecis et
Latinis docta, **psallere**, saltare elegantius quam necesse est probae, multa alia quae
instrumenta luxuriae sunt. sed ei cariora semper omnia quam decus atque pudicitia
fuerunt; pecuniae an famae minus parceret, haud facile discerneres. sed ea saepe antehac 5
fidem prodiderat, **creditum abiuraverat**, caedis conscia fuerat, luxuria atque inopia
praeceps abierat. verum ingenium eius haud **absurdum**: posse versus facere, iocum
movere, sermone uti vel modesto vel molli vel **procaci**; prorsus multae facetiae multusque
lepos inerat.

Line	3	psallere	to play the cithara
	4	instrumentum –i	concomitant, partner
	6	creditum abiurare	to deny a loan made to one
	7	praeceps abire	to go down hill
		absurdus –a –um	to be despised
	8	procax –acis	shameless
	9	lepos –oris	charm

1. What is meant by *virilis audaciae facinora* (1)?   2
2. In what respects was Sempronia lucky?   4
3. Lines 2-4: what accomplishments did she have, and what faults does Sallust
   find with them?   4,2
4. Show what constructions Sallust is using in lines 2-4 dependent on *docta*.   3
5. Lines 4-5 (*sed ei ... discerneres*): explain in your own words what faults are
   ascribed to her.   4
6. Account for the uses of the subjunctives *parceret* and *discerneres* in line 5.   2
7. verum (7): what does this word mean? (Be careful!)   1
8. What redeeming qualities did Sempronia have?   5
9. Account for the cases of *probae* (3), *pecuniae* (5), *sermone* (8).   3
10. Explain the use of the infinitive *posse* (7).   1
11. Why is *inerat* (9) singular?   1
12. Show, with close reference to the text, Sallust's attitude towards Sempronia.   4
13. Show, with close reference to the text, the main stylistic features of this passage.   <u>4</u>
                                                                                                        40

Caesar, *De Bello Civili* III. 42-43.

48 BC Pompey is encamped on a hill named Petra, near Dyrrachium. Caesar first tries to arrange his food supplies, before embarking on a siege of Pompey. Lissus is the town of the local tribe, the Parthini.

Caesar Lisso Parthinisque et omnibus castellis quod esset frumenti conquiri iussit. id erat 1
perexiguum cum ipsius agri natura, quod sunt loca aspera ac montuosa ac plerumque
frumento utuntur importato, tum quod Pompeius haec providerat et superioribus diebus
praedae loco Parthinos habuerat frumentumque omne conquisitum spoliatis eorum
domibus per equites in Petram comportarat. 5
    quibus rebus cognitis Caesar consilium capit ex loci natura. erant enim circum
castra Pompei permulti editi atque asperi colles. hos primum praesidiis tenuit castellaque
ibi communiit. inde, ut loci cuiusque natura ferebat, ex castello in castellum perducta
munitione circumvallare Pompeium instituit haec spectans, quod angusta re frumentaria
utebatur, quodque Pompeius multitudine equitum valebat, quo minore periculo undique 10
frumentum commeatumque exercitui supportare posset, simul uti pabulatione Pompeium
prohiberet equitatumque eius ad rem gerendam inutilem efficeret, tertio ut auctoritatem,
qua ille maxime apud exteras nationes niti videbatur, minueret, cum fama per orbem
terrarum percrebruisset illum a Caesare obsideri neque audere proelio dimicare.

1. (a) Why was there very little grain to be found locally? 4
    (b) What are the meanings of *cum … tum* (2-3) and *plerumque* (2)? 2
    (c) Account for the case of *frumenti* (1) and *praedae* (4). 2
    (d) Give the present infinitive of the verb of which *conquisitum* (4) is a compound. 1
    (e) What part of the verb is *comportarat* (5)? 1
2. What dictated the positioning of Caesar's forts and connecting fortifications? 2
3. In lines 9-10 (*valebat*) what two reasons does Caesar give for his strategy of enclosing Pompey? 2
4. In the rest of the passage Caesar cites three things he intends to achieve by this strategy. What are they? 2,3,4
5. Explain the use of *quo* (10). 1
6. Why is *videbatur* (13) indicative, but *percrebruisset* (14) subjunctive?
    Account for the tense of *percrebruisset*. (Be careful! This is all not as simple as it might appear.) 3
7. *percrebruisset* comes from *percrebresco*. What is the meaning of *-sco* ending a verbal stem? 1
8. Why is *loca* neuter in line 2, but masculine in line 8? 2
                                                       30

During the slave revolt of Spartacus (73-71 BC) Verres took action to preserve Sicily, and Cicero anticipates that the defence will use Verres' reputation as a general to over-ride the accusations against him. Cicero draws a comparison with Marcus Antonius' defence of Manius Aquilius.

non possum dissimulare, iudices; timeo ne C. Verres propter hanc eximiam virtutem in re   1
militari omnia, quae fecit, impune fecerit. venit enim mihi in mentem, in iudicio M'.
Aquili quantum auctoritatis, quantum momenti oratio M. Antoni habuisse existimata sit;
qui, ut erat in dicendo non solum sapiens, sed etiam fortis, causa prope perorata ipse
arripuit M'. Aquilium constituitque in conspectu omnium tunicamque eius a pectore   5
abscidit, ut **cicatrices** populus Romanus iudicesque aspicerent adverso corpore exceptas;
simul et de illo vulnere, quod ille in capite ab hostium duce acceperat, multa dixit eoque
adduxit eos, qui erant iudicaturi, vehementer ut vererentur, ne, quem virum fortuna ex
hostium telis eripuisset, cum sibi ipse non pepercisset, hic non ad populi Romani laudem,
sed ad iudicum crudelitatem videretur esse servatus. eadem nunc ab illis defensionis ratio   10
viaque temptatur, idem quaeritur. sit fur, sit sacrilegus, sit **flagitiorum** omnium
vitiorumque princeps; at est bonus imperator, at felix et ad dubia rei publicae tempora
reservandus.

Line	6	cicatrix –icis	scar
	11	flagitium	disgraceful behaviour

1.	What is Cicero's fear?	3
2.	Suggest an appropriate word to translate *momenti* (3).	1
3.	Lines 4-7: what was *fortis* about Antonius' method of defence?	3
4.	What were the particular points of importance about the scars and the head wound?	2
5.	In lines 8-10 what might be the jury's motive for acquitting Aquilius?	4
6.	What is the meaning of *cum* in line 9?	1
7.	Translate line 12 *sit fur* to *princeps* into idiomatic English. Pick out three features typical of a rhetorical style in this sentence.	3,3
8.	Account for the uses of the genitives *auctoritas* (3), *populi* (9).	2
9.	Compare the syntax and meanings of *dicendo* (4) and *reservandus* (13).	4
10.	Compare the uses of *ut* in lines 4, 6 and 8.	3
11.	Account for the subjunctives *existimata sit* (3), *eripuisset* (9).	2
12.	Give the present infinitives and meanings of *vererentur* (8), *pepercisset* (9).	4
		35

Aquilius was acquitted on the charge, also of maladministration in Sicily. He was later captured by Mithridates, and, as a commentary on the greed of the Romans, was executed by having molten gold poured down his throat!

Livy, XXX. 35.

Hannibal has been defeated at the Battle of Zama by Scipio. Despite the defeat the layout of his army and tactics are praised.

Hannibal cum paucis equitibus inter tumultum elapsus Hadrumentum perfugit, 1
omnia et integro proelio et inclinante acie, priusquam excederet pugna, expertus, et
confessione etiam Scipionis omniumque peritorum militiae illam laudem adeptus,
singulari arte aciem eo die instruxisse: elephantos in prima fronte, quorum **fortuitus**
impetus atque intolerabilis vis signa sequi et servare ordines, in quo plurimum spei 5
ponerent, Romanos prohiberent; deinde auxiliares ante Carthaginiensium aciem, ne
homines mixti ex **conluvione** omnium gentium, quos non fides teneret sed merces,
liberum receptum fugae haberent, simul primum ardorem atque impetum hostium
excipientes fatigarent ac, si nihil aliud, vulneribus suis ferrum hostile **hebetarent**: tum,
ubi omnis spes esset, milites Carthaginienses Afrosque, ut, omnibus rebus aliis pares, eo 10
quod integri cum fessis ac sauciis pugnarent, superiores essent: **Italicos** intervallo quoque
diremptos, incertos socii an hostes essent, in postremam aciem summotos. hoc **edito** velut
ultimo virtutis opere Hannibal cum Hadrumentum refugisset, **accitus**que inde
Carthaginem sexto ac tricesimo post anno, quam puer inde profectus erat, redisset, fassus
in curia est non proelio modo se sed bello victum, nec spem salutis alibi quam in pace 15
impetranda esse.

Line	4	fortuitus −a −um	random, haphazard
	7	conluvio	dregs, sweepings
	9	hebetare	to blunt
	11	Italicos	these Italians are fighting on the Carthaginian side.
	12	edere	to perform
	13	accire	to summon
	16	impetrare	to get by asking

1. What stages of the battle are described by *integro proelio et inclinante acie* (2)? — 2
2. Why were the elephants placed in the front rank? — 4
3. Line 5: to what does *quo* refer? — 1
4. Lines 6-9: what grounds did Hannibal have for doubting the determination of the auxiliaries, and why did he place them in front of the Carthaginians? — 3,5
5. Line 9: translate *si nihil aliud*, inserting an appropriate verb. — 2
6. What line of thought lay behind Hannibal's hope that the Carthaginians and Africans would prove the decisive force? — 4
7. Why did Hannibal place the Italians some distance in the rear? — 2
8. For how long had Hannibal been away from Carthage? — 1
9. What confession does Hannibal make to the Carthaginian senate? — 4
10. Account for the cases of *militiae* (3) and *spei* (5). — 2
11. What are the meanings of *eo* in lines 4 and 10? — 2
12. Accounts for the uses of the infinitives *instruxisse* (4) and *sequi* (5). — 2

13. Give the present infinitives of *elapsus* (1), *expertus* (2), *adeptus* (3), and
    fassus (14).   4
14. Account for the uses of the subjunctives *excederet* (2), *ponerent* (6),
    prohiberent (6), *essent* (11), *essent* (12).   5
15. Explain the uses of quam in lines 14 and 15.   2
                                                                                          ―――
                                                                                           45

Caesar, *De Bello Gallico* VII. 12.

When Caesar attacks Noviodunum, the citizens negotiate to surrender. But then Vercingetorix's cavalry arrive, and they change their minds.

Vercingetorix, ubi de Caesaris adventu cognovit, oppugnatione destitit atque obviam 1
Caesari proficiscitur. ille oppidum Biturigum positum in via Noviodunum oppugnare
instituerat. quo ex oppido cum legati ad eum venissent oratum ut sibi ignosceret suaeque
vitae consuleret, ut celeritate reliquas res conficeret, qua pleraque erat consecutus, arma
conferri, equos produci, obsides dari iubet. parte iam obsidum tradita, cum reliqua 5
administrarentur, centurionibus et paucis militibus intromissis qui arma iumentaque
conquirerent, equitatus hostium procul visus est, qui agmen Vercingetorigis antecesserat.
quem simul atque oppidani conspexerunt atque in spem auxili venerunt, clamore sublato
arma capere, portas claudere, murum complere coeperunt. centuriones in oppido, cum ex
significatione Gallorum novi aliquid ab eis iniri consili intellexissent, gladiis destrictis 10
portas occupaverunt suosque omnes incolumes receperunt.

1.	What did Vercingetorix do when he heard about Caesar's arrival?	2
2.	Explain the syntax and meaning of *oratum* (3).	2
3.	What requests did the envoys of the Bituriges make?	2
4.	What instructions did Caesar give, and what was his intention?	3,3
5.	To what extent were Caesar's instructions carried out?	3
6.	What is the antecedent of *quem* (8)?	1
7.	*oppidani conspexerunt* (8): how did the townspeople react to the sight? How does Caesar give an effect of noise and rushing to line 9?	5,2
8.	What did the centurions realise, and what did they do as a result?	2,4
9.	Account for the subjunctives *consuleret* (4), *conficeret* (4), *conquirerent* (7).	3
10.	Account for the cases of *Caesari* (2), *aliquid* (10), *consili* (10).	3
		35

Seneca, *Epistulae* 77. 5-9.

Seneca describes to Lucilius the suicide of their friend, Marcellinus.

Tullius Marcellinus, morbo non insanabili correptus sed longo et molesto et multa   1
imperante, coepit deliberare de morte. convocavit complures amicos. unusquisque aut,
quia timidus erat, id illi suadebat quod sibi suasisset, aut, quia **adulator** et blandus, id
consilium dabat quod deliberanti gratius fore suspicabatur; amicus noster Stoicus, homo
egregius et, ut verbis illum quibus laudari dignus est laudem, vir fortis ac strenuus,   5
videtur mihi optime illum cohortatus. sic enim coepit: 'noli, mi Marcelline, torqueri
tamquam de re magna deliberes. non est res magna vivere; omnes servi tui vivunt, omnia
animalia; magnum est honeste mori, prudenter, fortiter.'
    non opus erat suasore Marcellino, sed **adiutore**; servi parere nolebant. primum
amicus noster detraxit illis metum, et indicavit tunc **familiam periculum adire** cum   10
incertum esset an mors domini voluntaria fuisset. deinde ipsum Marcellinum admonuit
non esse inhumanum, quemadmodum cena peracta **reliquiae** circumstantibus dividantur,
sic peracta vita aliquid porrigi iis qui totius vitae ministri fuissent. minutas itaque
summulas distribuit flentibus servis et illos ultro consolatus est. non fuit illi opus ferro,
non sanguine; triduo cibo abstinuit et in ipso cubiculo poni **tabernaculum** iussit; **solium**   15
deinde illatum est, in quo diu iacuit et calida aqua **subinde** suffusa paulatim defecit, ut
aiebat, non sine quadam voluptate.

Line	3	adulator –ris	flatterer, sycophant
	9	adiutor –ris	ie. to help him die
	10	familiam periculum adire	it was the law that, if a slave murdered his master, all the slaves in the house were put to death.
	12	reliquiae –arum	left-overs
	14	summula –ae	small sum of money
	15	tabernaculum –i	tent (to keep in the vapours)
		solium –ii	bath-tub
	16	subinde	repeatedly

1. What information are we given about Marcellinus' illness?   3
2. What were the two types of advice given to Marcellinus in lines 2-4?   4
3. Translate *ut verbis illum quibus laudari dignus est laudem* (5).   3
4. Which Latin words tell you whether Seneca agrees with his friend's advice?   1
5. How does Seneca use word order for emphasis in lines 6-8? What other tech-
    niques is he using here for effect?   2,2
6. Under what circumstances does the friend say slaves came into danger?   3
7. Explain the analogy which the friend uses to advise Marcellinus to give his
    slaves presents.   4
8. What is the point of *ultro* in line 14?   1
9. Describe the way that Marcellinus died.   4
10. *suasore* and *adiutore* (9) are formed in the same way. Give another noun from
    the passage of the same formation. How are these nouns formed, and what do
    all such nouns have in common in terms of meaning?   3
11. Account for the cases of *illis* (10) and *illi* (14).   2
12. Account for the subjunctives *suasisset* (3), *deliberes* (7); *fuissent* (13).   3
                                                                                          ___
                                                                                           35

Cicero, *In Catilinam* II. 7. 14-15.

November 63 BC Caticline has abandoned Rome, pretending to go into exile in Massilia, but in fact going to join his rebel army in Etruria. Cicero has assembled the people in the Forum, and explains what has happened and justifies his actions.

o condicionem miseram non modo administrandae, verum etiam conservandae rei 1
publicae! nunc si L. Catilina consiliis laboribus periculis meis circumclusus ac debilitatus
subito pertimuerit, sententiam mutaverit, deseruerit suos, consilium belli faciendi
abiecerit, ex hoc cursu sceleris et belli iter ad fugam atque in exilium converterit, non ille
a me spoliatus armis audaciae, non obstupefactus ac perterritus mea diligentia, non de 5
spe conatuque depulsus, sed indemnatus, innocens in exilium eiectus a consule vi et
minis dicetur, et erunt qui illum, si hoc fecerit, non improbum, sed miserum, me non
diligentissimum consulem, sed crudelissimum tyrannum existimari velint. est mihi tanti,
Quirites, huius invidiae falsae atque iniquae tempestatem subire dummodo a vobis huius
horribilis belli ac nefarii periculum depellatur. dicatur sane eiectus esse a me, dummodo 10
eat in exilium: sed, mihi credite, non est iturus.

1.	(a) What does Cicero consider to be a pitiful task?	2
	(b) What is the meaning of *verum*?	1
2.	In line 2 what difference is there in the meaning of *meis* as applied to *consiliis* and to *periculis*?	1
3.	What possible changes does Cicero see in Catiline's course of action in lines 3-4?	4
4.	In lines 5-8:	
	(a) what difference is there between the way Cicero sees himself and Catiline, and the way some wish them to be judged?	7
	(b) why is *velint* subjunctive?	1
5.	Translate lines 10-11: *dicatur sane eiectus esse a me, dummodo eat in exilium.*	3
6.	What difference in meaning does Cicero produce by writing *non est iturus* rather than *non ibit*?	1
7.	Explain the metaphors *armis audaciae* (5) and *invidiae tempestatem* (9).	4
8.	Account for the cases of *condicionem* (1), *armis* (5), *mihi* (8), *tanti* (8).	4
9.	Explain briefly and quote from this passage one example each of antithesis, anaphora, tricolon, alliteration, hendiadys, asyndeton.	<u>12</u>
		40

Livy, I. 49.

Tarquinius, seventh and last king of Rome (trad. 534-510 BC) has gained power by the assassination of his father-in-law, King Servius. This passage describes how he earned the name 'Superbus'.

inde L. Tarquinius regnare incipit, cui Superbo cognomen facta indiderunt, quia **socerum** 1
gener sepultura prohibuit, Romulum quoque inseptultum perisse dictitans, primoresque
patrum, quos Servi rebus favisse credebat, interfecit; conscius deinde male quaerendi
regni ab se ipso adversus se exemplum capi posse, armatis corpus circumsaepsit; neque
enim ad ius regni quicquam praeter vim habebat, ut qui neque populi iussu neque 5
auctoribus patribus regnaret. eo accedebat ut ei in caritate civium nihil spei reponenti
metu regnum tutandum esset. quem ut pluribus iniceret, **cognitiones** capitalium rerum
sine consiliis per se solus exercebat, perque eam causam occidere, in exsilium agere,
bonis **multare** poterat non suspectos modo aut invisos sed unde nihil aliud quam praedam
sperare posset. praecipue ita patrum numero imminuto statuit nullos in patres legere, quo 10
contemptior paucitate ipsa ordo esset minusque per se nihil agi indignaretur.

Line	1	socer –eri	father-in-law
	2	gener –eri	son-in-law
	7	cognitio –onis	trial
	9	multare + abl. of the penalty	to punish

1. What did Tarquinius do to Servius in line 2, and on what grounds did he justify it? Why has Livy used the words *socerum gener* and placed them in this word order?   1,2,2

2. What is the force of *-ito* in *dictito* (2)?   1

3. What does *rebus* mean in line 3?   1

4. Why did he surround himself with a bodyguard?   3

5. Line 5: what was the basis of Tarquinius' right to rule?   1

6. What would have been proper grounds for his ruling? What is the meaning of *ut qui* + subjunctive? Account for the case of *patribus* (6).   2,1,1

7. Why did Tarquinius have to keep the throne by means of fear? Account for the cases of *ei* (6) and *spei* (6).   2,2

8. Lines 7-10: explain how Tarquinius made fear widespread. Pick out three stylistic features or idioms from this sentence.   8,3

9. What effect did this have on the senate, and why did Tarquinius decide to appoint no new senators?   1,3

10. Why must *quo* be used in lines 10-11 and where, earlier in the passage, does Livy break this rule? Explain the grammar and syntax of *agi*.   2,2

11. Compare the syntax and meanings of *quaerendi* (3) and *tutandum* (7).   <u>2</u>
    40

Cicero, *Philippic* II. x. 23-24.

Mark Antony has accused Cicero of alienating Pompey from Caesar, so causing the Civil War. Cicero has replied that Antony has the timing, rather than the basic fact, wrong. Bibulus was Consul with Caesar in 59 BC.

ego M. Bibulo, praestantissimo cive, consule, nihil praetermisi, quantum facere enitique 1
potui, quin Pompeium a Caesaris coniunctione avocarem. in quo Caesar felicior fuit; ipse
enim Pompeium a mea familiaritate diiunxit. postea vero quam se totum Pompeius
Caesari tradidit, quid ego illum ab eo distrahere conarer? stulti erat sperare: suadere
impudentis. duo tamen tempora inciderunt, quibus aliquid contra Caesarem Pompeio 5
suaserim. ea velim **reprehendas**, si potes: unum, ne quinquenni **imperium** Caesari
prorogaret: alterum, ne pateretur **ferri, ut** absentis **eius ratio haberetur**. quorum si
utrumvis persuasissem, in has miserias numquam incidissemus. atque idem ego, cum iam
opes omnes et suas et populi Romani Pompeius ad Caesarem detulisset seroque ea sentire
coepisset, quae ego multo ante provideram, inferrique patriae bellum viderem nefarium, 10
pacis concordiae compositionis auctor esse non destiti, meaque illa vox est nota multis:
'utinam, Cn. Pompei, cum C. Caesare societatem aut numquam coisses, aut numquam
diremisses! fuit alterum gravitatis, alterum prudentiae tuae.' haec mea, M. Antoni,
semper et de Pompeio et de republica consilia fuerunt.

Line 6	suaserim	a consecutive subjunctive
	reprehendere	to criticise
	imperium	his governorship in Gaul
7	prorogare	to extend
	ferre ut	to propose a law that
	eius rationem habere	to allow him to stand for office

1. In lines 1-3 in what way was Caesar more successful than Cicero? 3
2. In line 3 what is the use of *quam* and in line 4 what does *quid* mean? 2
3. *duo tempora* (5): what were the two occasions? 2
4. What is the point of the change from *suaserim* (6) to the compound form *persuasissem* (8)? 1
5. What is the force or meaning of *idem* (8)? 1
6. What were the circumstances in lines 8-10 under which Cicero continually urged peace and reconciliation? 5
7. What is the meaning of *vox* in line 11? 1
8. What is Cicero's wish in lines 12-13? 2
9. Why might you have expected *fuisset* rather than *fuit* in line 13? Why has Cicero written an indicative? 2
10. Account for the subjunctives *conarer* (4), *velim* (6), *reprehendas* (6). 3
11. Account for the cases of *consule* (1), *stulti* (4), *quibus* (5), *multo* (10). 4
12. Pick out four points typical of a rhetorical style of writing. 4
   30

Seneca, *Epistulae* 47. 11-17.

Seneca writes to Lucilius on the treatment of slaves.

haec praecepti mei summa est: sic cum inferiore vivas, quemadmodum tecum superiorem 1
velis vivere. quotiens in mentem venerit quantum tibi in servum liceat, veniat in mentem
tantundem in te domino tuo licere. 'at ego' inquis 'nullum habeo dominum'. **bona aetas
est:** forsitan habebis. nescis qua aetate Hecuba servire coeperit, qua Croesus, qua Darei
mater, qua Platon, qua Diogenes? vive cum servo clementer, comiter quoque, et in 5
sermonem illum admitte et in consilium et in **convictum.** 'quid ergo? omnes servos
admovebo mensae meae?' non magis quam omnes liberos. quidam cenent tecum, quia
digni sunt, quidam, ut sint. **non est,** mi Lucili, **quod** amicum tantum in foro et in curia
quaeras: si diligenter attenderis, et domi invenies. quemadmodum stultus est qui equum
empturus non ipsum inspicit, sed **stratum** eius ac **frenos,** sic stultissimus est qui hominem 10
aut ex veste aut ex **condicione,** quae vestis modo nobis circumdata est, aestimat. 'servus
est.' sed fortasse liber animo. 'servus est.' hoc illi nocebit? ostende quis non sit: alius
libidini servit, alius avaritiae, alius ambitioni, omnes spei, omnes timori.

Line	3-4	bona aetas est	'you are still young'
	6	convictus –us	dining together
	8	non est quod	there is no reason why
	10	stratum –i	saddle
		freni –orum	reins
	11	condicio –onis	position in life

1. What is the main point of Seneca's rule? Give an equivalent English proverb
   or maxim?   3,2
2. What is Lucilius to bear in mind in lines 2-3?   3
3. Account for the tense of *venerit* (2).   1
4. What is the point of Seneca's list of people in lines 4-5?   2
5. What is Seneca's answer to the idea of inviting all your slaves to dine with you?
   What two groups should be invited?   2,2
6. Explain the analogy regarding the horse in lines 9-11.   5
7. What answers does Seneca offer to the supposed protest "But he is a slave"?   5
8. Summarise Seneca's argument in this passage.   4
9. What are the meanings in this passage of these words: *forsitan* (4), *tantum* (8),
   modo (11)?   3
10. Account for the uses of the subjunctives *velis* (2), *veniat* (2), *coeperit* (4).   3
                                                                                    ——
                                                                                    35

Livy, V. 36. 7-11.

387 BC A migrating horde of Gauls is threatening Clusium and demanding land on which to settle. The people of Clusium have asked Rome for help; the Senate has refused military aid, but sent the three Fabii brothers – the Fabian family was one of the most powerful and influential in Rome – as envoys to negotiate with the Gauls. But tempers have flared; violence has broken out; the envoys have taken up arms, and Quintus Fabius has killed the Gallic chieftain.

Fabium spolia ducis legentem Galli agnovere, perque totam aciem Romanum legatum 1
esse signum datum est. omissa inde in Clusinos ira, recepti canunt minantes Romanis.
     erant qui extemplo Romam eundum censerent; vicere seniores, ut legati prius
mitterentur questum iniurias postulatumque ut pro iure gentium violato Fabii dederentur.
legati Gallorum cum ea sicut erant mandata exposuissent, senatui nec factum placebat 5
Fabiorum et ius postulare barbari videbantur; sed ne id quod placebat decerneretur in
tantae nobilitatis viris **ambitio** obstabat. itaque ne **penes** ipsos culpa esset cladis forte
Gallico bello acceptae, cognitionem de postulatis Gallorum ad populum reiciunt; ubi
tanto plus gratia atque opes valuere ut quorum de poena agebatur tribuni militum in
insequentem annum crearentur. quo facto haud secus quam dignum erat infensi Galli 10
bellum palam minantes ad suos redeunt.

Line 7	ambitio –onis + in + abl.	a desire to please …
	penes + acc.	in the control of, the responsibility of

1. In lines 1-2
   (a) what was Fabius doing when the Gauls recognised him?   1
   (b) what was the reaction of the Gauls to this recognition?   3
   (c) account for the case of *receptui*.   1
2. In line 3 what is the first proposal? Why is *censerent* subjunctive?   2,1
3. What do the elders propose? Explain the syntax of *questum*.   4,2
4. In lines 5-7 what is the reaction of the Senate to the Gallic protest?   4
5. Why does the Senate hand over the decision on the Gallic demands to the people?   3
6. In lines 8-10:
   (a) what is the meaning here of *ubi*?   1
   (b) account for the case of *tanto*.   1
   (c) what was the decision of the people, and why did they come to this decision?   2,2
7. How did the Gauls react to the decision of the people? What is Livy's view
   on the Gallic reaction?   2,1
                                                                                                         30

Tacitus, *Annals* I. 51.

14 AD After the army on the Rhine mutinied, Germanicus (Caesar) quelled the mutiny and gave the soldiers the chance to expiate their guilt by an attack across the Rhine on the Marsi.

Caesar avidas legiones quo latior **populatio** foret quattuor in **cuneos** dispertit: 1
quinquaginta milium spatium ferro flammisque pervastat. non sexus, non aetas
miserationem attulit: profana simul et sacra et celeberrimum illis gentibus templum quod
Tanfanae vocabant solo aequantur. sine vulnere milites, qui semisomnos, inermos aut
palantes ceciderant. excivit ea caedes Bructeros, Tubantes, Usipetes, saltusque, per quos 5
exercitui regressus, insedere. quod notum duci incessitque itineri et proelio. pars equitum
et auxiliariae cohortes ducebant, mox prima legio, et mediis impedimentis sinistrum latus
unetvicesimani, dextrum quintani clausere, vicesima legio terga firmavit, post ceteri
sociorum. sed hostes, donec agmen per saltus **porrigeretur**, immoti, dein latera et frontem
modice adsultantes, tota vi novissimos incurrere. turbanturque densis Germanorum 10
catervis leves cohortes, cum Caesar advectus ad vicesimanos voce magna hoc illud
tempus obliterandae seditionis clamitabat; pergerent, properarent culpam in decus
vertere. exarsere animis unoque impetu perruptum hostem redigunt in aperta caeduntque.
quietum inde iter, fidensque recentibus ac priorum oblitus, miles in hibernis locatur.

Line	1	populatio –onis	devastation
		cuneus –i	(here) flying column
	5	palari	to wander, be scattered
	9	porrigere	to stretch out

1. What was the mood of the soldiers?   1
2. What construction is introduced by *quo* (1), and why does *quo* have to be used here?   2
3. How widespread was the devastation, and how in lines 2-4 does Tacitus emphasise its severity?   1,5
4. Why were there no casualties among the soldiers?   2
5. What part of the verb is *insedere* (6)?   1
6. In lines 6-9 what was the Roman order of march? How does Tacitus avoid monotony in this list?   4,3
7. In lines 9-11 what were the Germans' tactics, and how successful were they initially?   3,1
8. What is the theme of Germanicus' words of encouragement?   2
9. How successful were Germanicus' words?   3
10. Why are *porrigeretur* (9) and *pergerent* (12) subjunctive, and *clamitabat* (12) indicative?   3
11. Account for the cases of *exercitui* (6) and *itineri* (6).   2
12. Give the present infinitives and their meanings of *ceciderant* (5), *advectus* (11), *oblitus* (14).   3
13. How does Tacitus bring variety and vigour to his narrative (do not use again any examples from question 6)?   <u>4</u>

                                                                   40

Seneca, *Epistulae* 53. 1-3.

Seneca describes an uncomfortable experience at sea.

quid non potest mihi persuaderi, cui persuasum est ut navigarem? solvi mari languido. 1
erat sine dubio caelum grave sordidis nubibus, sed putavi tam pauca milia a **Parthenope**
usque Puteolos **surripi** posse, quamvis dubio et impendente caelo. itaque quo celerius
evaderem, protinus per altum ad **Nesida** direxi cursum praecisurus omnes sinus. cum iam
eo processissem ut **mea** nihil **interesset** utrum irem an redirem, primum aequalitas illa 5
quae me **corruperat** periit. nondum erat tempestas, sed iam inclinatio maris ac **subinde**
crebrior fluctus. coepi gubernatorem rogare ut me in aliquo litore exponeret. aiebat ille
aspera esse et **importuosa** nec quicquam se aeque in tempestate timere quam terram.
peius autem nausea vexabar quam ut mihi periculum **succurreret**. institi itaque
gubernatori et illum coegi petere litus. cuius ut viciniam attigimus, non exspecto ut 10
quicquam ex praeceptis Vergilii fiat, 'obvertunt pelago proras' aut 'ancora de prora
iacitur'; mitto me in mare.

Line	2	Parthenope (abl. Pathenope)	Naples
	3	surripere	to snatch, steal
	4	Nesis (acc. Nesida)	an island between Naples and Puteoli
	5	mea interest	it matters to me
	6	corrumpere	to deceive
		subinde	continually
	8	importuosus	without a harbour
	10	succurrere	to enter one's thoughts

1. Explain in your own words the point of Seneca's question. — 3
2. Describe the state of the sea and weather when Seneca set sail. Why does *solvere* mean "to set sail"? — 3,1
3. What is the point of this metaphorical use of *surripi* (3)? — 1
4. Explain the use of *quo* in line 3. — 1
5. Describe the course Seneca is taking. How far has he gone when trouble first starts brewing? — 2,2
6. Why does the helmsman refuse to put Seneca ashore? Why are *aspera* and *importuosa* neuter plural? — 3,1
7. Why did Seneca insist that the helmsman put him ashore? — 2
8. What do the quotations from Vergil tell you about the method of mooring a ship? — 2
9. How does Seneca bring a sense of drama and humour to the way he got ashore? — 3
10. Compare the uses of *ut* in lines 5, 9 and 10 (×2). — 4
11. Compare the uses of *quam* in lines 8 and 9. — 2
    30

Caesar, *De Bello Gallico* VII. 30-31.

After the disastrous loss of their town of Avaricum, Vercingetorix, commander in chief of the Gauls, bravely faced them, and promised to make good the disaster and win over the rest of the country to their side. His position was strengthened by his boldness and by the fact that he had opposed the defence of Avaricum.

fuit haec oratio non ingrata Gallis, et maxime, quod ipse animo non defecerat tanto 1
accepto incommodo neque se in occultum abdiderat et conspectum multitudinis fugerat;
plusque animo providere et praesentire existimabatur, quod re integra primo
incendendum Avaricum, post deserendum censuerat. itaque ut reliquorum imperatorum
res adversae auctoritatem minuunt, sic huius ex contrario dignitas incommodo accepto in 5
dies augebatur. primum eo tempore Galli castra munire instituerunt, et sic sunt animo
consternati homines insueti laboris ut omnia quae imperarentur sibi patienda
existimarent.
nec minus quam est pollicitus Vercingetorix animo laborabat ut reliquas civitates
adiungeret, atque eas donis pollicitationibusque **alliciebat**. qui Avarico expugnato 10
refugerant, armandos vestiendosque curat; simul, ut deminutae copiae redintegrarentur,
imperat certum numerum militum civitatibus, **quem** et quam ante diem in castra adduci
velit, sagittariosque omnes, quorum erat permagnus numerus in Gallia, conquiri et ad se
mitti iubet. his rebus celeriter id quod Avarici deperierat expletur.

Line	7	consternare	to alarm
	10	allicere	to tempt
	12	quem	= quem numerum

1.	Why were the Gauls particularly impressed by Vercingetorix's speech?	4
2.	Lines 3-4: why was Vercingetorix thought to have foresight?	3
3.	Lines 4-6 (*augebatur*): explain the point that Caesar is making in these lines.	4
4.	What unprecedented act did the Gauls now do, and what does Caesar regard as a sign of how alarmed they were?	1,3
5.	Compare the syntax and meanings of *ut ... sic* (4-5) and *sic ... ut* (6-7).	4
6.	How did Vercingetorix set about winning over the other tribes?	2
7.	What is the antecedent of *qui* (10)?	1
8.	Lines 10 (*qui*) – 14: how did Vercingetorix raise a new army?	6
9.	Comment on the gender of *diem* (12).	1
10.	Translate line 14 *his rebus* to *expletur*.	3
11.	What is the force or meaning of the prefix on *redintegrarentur* (11), *permagnus* (13)?	2
12.	Account for the moods of *redintegrarentur* (11), *velit* (13), *erat* (13).	1,1,2
13.	Comment on the cases with *impero* in lines 7 and 12.	2
14.	Compare the uses of *patienda* (7) and *armandos* (11).	2
15.	Account for the cases of *re integra* (3), *Avaricum* (4), *tempore* (6), *laboris* (7).	4
16.	Give the present infinitive active of the simple verbs of which these are compounds: *abdiderat* (2), *instituerunt* (6), *conquiri* (13), *deperierat* (14).	4
		50

Quintillian, *Institutio Oratoria* XII. 1. 14-18.

'non posse oratorem esse nisi virum bonum.' *Quintillian discusses the proposition that an orator must be, as defined by Marcus Cato, 'a good man, skilled in speaking'.*

nunc de iis dicendum est quae mihi quasi **conspiratione** quadam vulgi **reclamari** videntur: 1
'orator ergo Demosthenes non fuit? atqui malum virum accepimus. non Cicero? atqui
huius quoque mores multi reprenderunt.' quid agam? magna responsi invidia subeunda
est, mitigandae sunt prius aures. mihi enim nec Demosthenes tam gravi morum dignus
videtur invidia ut omnia quae in eum ab inimicis congesta sunt credam, cum et 5
pulcherrima eius in re publica consilia et finem vitae clarum legam, nec **M. Tullio**
defuisse video in ulla parte civis optimi **voluntatem**. testimonio est actus nobilissime
consulatus, integerrime provincia administrata et repudiatus **vigintiviratus**, et civilibus
bellis quae in aetatem eius gravissima inciderunt neque spe neque metu **declinatus**
animus, quo minus optimis se partibus, id est rei publicae iungeret. parum fortis videtur 10
quibusdam, quibus optime respondit ipse 'non se timidum in suscipiendis sed in
providendis periculis'; quod probavit morte quoque ipsa, quam praestantissimo suscepit
animo. quod si defuit his viris summa virtus, sic quaerentibus an oratores fuerint
respondebo quo modo Stoici, si interrogentur an sapiens Zeno an Cleanthes an
Chrysippus ipse, respondeant: magnos quidem illos ac venerabiles, non tamen id quod 15
natura hominis summum habet consecutos.

Line	1	conspiratio	agreement, consensus
		reclamare	to object to
	6	Marcus Tullius	Cicero
	7	voluntas	attitude, outlook
	8	vigintiviratus	membership of the Campanian commission
	9	declinare	to turn away, deter

1. Lines 1-2: what does he say that he must now discuss? 1
2. Translate *atqui malum virum accepimus* (2). 2
3. What objection is made to Cicero? 2
4. Explain what Quintillian means in lines 3-4 (*magna ... aures*). 4
5. What are the grounds of Quintillian's defences of (a) Demosthenes, (b) Cicero? 3,2
6. Comment on the word order of line 6 (*pulcherrima ... clarum*), and its effect. 2
7. How did Cicero demonstrate his *voluntatem* (7)? 6
8. What criticism is made of Cicero in line 10-11? 1
9. How did Cicero prove this criticism unjustified? 2
10. What would the Stoics say about Zeno, Cleanthes and Chrysippus? 4
11. Explain the idiom by which *summum* (16) is place inside the relative clause. 2
12. Account for the cases of *morum* (4), *invidia* (5), *Tullio* (6), *testimonio* (7), *quaerentibus* (13). 5
13. Account for the uses of the subjunctive in *agam* (3), *legam* (6), *fuerint* (13), *respondeant* (15). 4

40